SPHERE RIGH

SPHERE RIGHTS GUIDES
Series Editor: Andrew Arden

THE DISABLED PERSONS HANDBOOK

JAN LUBA

SPHERE REFERENCE

A SPHERE BOOK

First published in Great Britain
by Sphere Books Ltd 1989

Typeset in Plantin by Leaper & Gard Ltd, Bristol, England
Printed and bound in Great Britain by
The Guernsey Press

ISBN 0-7474-02124

Sphere Books Ltd
A Division of
Macdonald & Co (Publishers) Ltd
27 Wrights Lane
London W8 5TZ
A Maxwell Pergamon Publishing Corporation plc

Contents

Contents

Contents

Disabled Dependants Allowance

Contents

Publisher's Note

The law on disabled persons can change at short notice.
This book describes the law as at April 1st 1989.
You should always check if what it says is still correct.

Introduction

This book is written for people with disabilities, people
raising children who have disabilities and people caring
for disabled adults. It is not targetted at any particular
form of disability. Nor does it attempt to define disability.
If you *feel* that you are in any way disabled or are caring
for a disabled person I hope that you can find something
in this book of interest to you.

This book is intended to provide an *outline* of the rights
people in Britain have if they are disabled. You will not
find every small detail covered in full. The aim of this
book is more to try to help you know better what is available and how to go about obtaining it. Wherever possible
it directs you to a source of further information and
advice which can provide more detailed information. If
you feel that you also want a very detailed guide to read
with this one I would strongly recommend the excellent
Disability Rights Handbook from the Disability Alliance
(address on page 134) which can seem dauntingly detailed
but which you might find easier to use after reading this
book.

The arrangements made for the disabled in this country
can hardly be described as generous. Taken individually it would seem that the benefits and social advantages
made available to disabled people are paltry. One aim of
this book is to demonstrate just how wide a range of
support and assistance is in fact available. A disabled
person qualifying for one sort of provision might thereby
become entitled to many more benefits and allowances.
But the social rights of the disabled (just like the social
rights of the population as a whole) receive little publicity,
and very little encouragement or advice is directed at

making sure everything available is applied for or claimed.

Most of the rights of the disabled emerge from duties owed by large organizations like the Departments of Health and Social Security and the Social Service Departments of local authorities. Dealing with bureaucracies is never easy and if you are disabled it can be doubly difficult. In this book I refer frequently to sources of help and advice which can provide the assistance sometimes needed to get administrators to focus on and deal with your rights. The details of these organizations, many concerned exclusively with supporting disabled people, are given in Chapter 11 at the end of this book. They are there to be used. Don't hesitate to contact them if you think you need help in pursuing the rights outlined in the earlier chapters.

In late 1988 the Government had begun to receive the results of the biggest national survey ever undertaken into the needs of the disabled in Britain. When this book was completed the details on the financial circumstances of the 6.2 million disabled adults in Britain were released. These showed that many thousands of disabled people were living on lower incomes and in poorer circumstances than their non-disabled neighbours through simple lack of knowledge of their rights or a failure to claim them. This book aims to make a contribution to the eradication of that problem by setting out in simple and clear terms what help is available and how it can be obtained. At every possible point it encourages claims to be made. The reader will recognize that this may sometimes lead to disappointment as the detailed conditions may rule out a particular claim, but the message is that this 'cost' is worth bearing to achieve the proper rights and compensation for disabled people entitled to them.

This book deals primarily with the position of disabled

people in England, Scotland and Wales. Readers in Northern Ireland may find it helpful to contact:

Northern Ireland Council on Disability
2 Annadale Ave
Belfast
BT7 3JR
Telephone: 0232 491011

1. Compensation for Disability

Can I get compensation for the cause of my disability?

Whether you can get compensation depends on how your disability was caused and how long ago it happened. In the United Kingdom there is no automatic right to compensation for disability – you can't qualify for compensation simply because you are disabled. In other countries there is such 'no fault' compensation provision, but here you usually need to prove that someone or something was actually to blame for your disability before you are entitled to compensation. There are some exceptions under which you can get compensation whether someone is to blame or not and these are described below.

If you are not covered by the exceptions, you will only receive compensation if you prove that your disability is someone else's fault. Making a compensation claim is fairly straightforward but you will find it useful to have professional advice. Your local Citizens' Advice Bureau (or one of the other helping agencies mentioned in Chapter 11) will be able to direct you to solicitors who specialize in compensation claims. If you were injured in an accident, they will give you details of the Accident Legal Advice Service under which inexpensive initial legal advice can be provided. Otherwise, if you are on a modest or low income, you will get help with any lawyer's fees under a scheme called *legal aid* which the solicitor will explain. (More details are given in *The Lawyer–Client Handbook* available in this series.)

You need to act fairly promptly because the normal rule is that claims for compensation must be lodged within three years of the harm being caused.

How does claiming compensation work?

If you have a serious or lasting disability it is worth getting the help of a solicitor or other legal adviser at the outset. The legal adviser will arrange for a specialist and your own GP to provide medical reports about your disability and its cause and then take up your case.

If there is a reasonable chance of showing that some other person or institution (e.g. a company or a hospital) is responsible for causing your disability (or making an existing disability worse) your solicitor will write to them claiming compensation on your behalf. If they are an official body, company or professional person the claim will probably be passed to an insurer with whom they have taken out a policy to protect themselves against compensation claims. Your solicitor will then correspond further with the insurance company or uninsured person on 'the other side'.

Two aspects of the compensation claim need to be settled. First, is liability admitted? (i.e. does the 'other side' admit it is partly or wholly to blame for your disability?). Second, how much compensation should be paid?

If liability is not admitted, the case may well have to go to court. If liability is admitted, further dealings will focus on the amount of compensation to be paid.

Most compensation claims are 'settled' by agreement between your solicitor (acting on your behalf) and the other side. You must be satisfied with the terms of the settlement before the solicitor can agree on your behalf. If you feel that the proposed settlement offers too little compensation, ask your solicitor to get a specialist opinion from a barrister or take a second opinion yourself from a different solicitor.

If liability is not admitted or compensation cannot be agreed, the claim will have to be resolved in court. The case might take many months or years before a hearing can be arranged. Your solicitor should be making arrangements for you to receive interim payments from the other side if the argument is simply over how much you should be paid.

While all this is going on you will have to claim legal aid to help cover your lawyer's fees or be paying them yourself. If you win the case the other side will be ordered to pay some of your costs. Because this will not cover your whole legal bill, some of your compensation money will be kept back by your lawyers to settle their own fees. It is very important to find out how much this will be before you agree to any settlement.

How much compensation can I claim?

Because the extent and effect of disability is different in every case there is no simple way of working out how much compensation you can claim or should receive. Lawyers base their advice about the appropriate figure on earlier court cases and settlements for similar injuries. As disability can vary from the minor to the very severe, compensation also varies from one pound to one million pounds. You will have to rely to a large extent on the legal advice you receive. Compensation will usually be worked out to cover such things as loss of earnings, reduction of life expectancy, costs of additional care or domestic needs, and general compensation for the effect of the disability itself.

If you are advised that your compensation claim will be worth less than £1000 you could make the claim yourself. If the other side do not pay up you can take action in the local County Court under the Small Claims procedure. This means that whether you win or lose you will not have to pay costs of lawyers involved. You can get a free booklet about using the Small Claims procedure from your local County Court office (see under Courts in the phone book).

If I was injured in a crime, how do I claim compensation?

The first thing to consider is the possibility of claiming against the criminal. If a person has been convicted of the offence which caused your disability it is possible for the criminal court to order the offender to pay you compensation at the same time as imposing the sentence for the crime. If you want to seek compensation in this way, mention it to the police investigating the crime.

If the criminal courts do not order the offender to provide compensation, the next possibility is to claim compensation from the offender in the ordinary way described above (pages 4–6). The practical difficulty is that usually criminal offenders have insufficient money to make claiming against them worthwhile and if they have been imprisoned they will not even have an income. In other cases the offender is never found. However, if the offender is known and relatively wealthy it is well worth taking advice about claiming compensation from him or her.

Because these possibilities are not usually practical, in most cases where disability has been caused by crime there is a separate *Criminal Injuries Compensation Scheme.* You can make a claim under this scheme if you were injured in the course of crime (or in trying to prevent one or helping the police stop a suspected criminal) whether or not anyone was arrested or convicted. You cannot claim if you suffered only very minor injuries (for which only a small amount of compensation would be paid) or if you were disabled in a traffic accident (but see below).

Full details of the scheme are available in the free booklet *Victims of Crimes of Violence,* available from the Criminal Injuries Compensation Board at Whittington House, 19 Alfred Place, London WC1E 7LG (tel: 01 636 2812). It costs nothing to apply and compensation available is assessed on the same basis as for other compensation claims (see above) so it may amount to many thousands of pounds.

If I was injured in a traffic accident, how do I claim compensation?

If you were covered by an insurance policy at the time of the accident you should claim on that policy. Your insurance company will pay you the necessary compensation and themselves try to recover compensation from the person who caused the accident.

If you were not insured against such accidents, e.g. you were a pedestrian accidentally run down by a motorist, you should make a claim for compensation against the person responsible in the way described at the beginning of this chapter.

If you were deliberately run down, you should claim in the same way as if you had been injured in any other crime (see above) and in particular make a claim under the Criminal Injuries Compensation Scheme.

If the person responsible cannot be traced or was not insured, a compensation scheme run by the Motor Insurance Bureau (MIB) applies. This will pay compensation equivalent to what you would have received if you had claimed in the normal way (see above). Claims must be put in within three years of the date of the accident. You can get all the details from the MIB, 78 Hatton Garden, London EC1N 8JQ (tel: 01 242 0033).

If I was injured while at work, how do I claim compensation?

The procedures involved in claiming compensation for disabilities caused by injuries at work and occupational diseases are described in Chapter 2.

If I was disabled as a result of medical treatment, how do I claim compensation?

The basic principle for all compensation claims – that the injury resulted from someone else's fault – applies equally to claims arising from medical treatments or accidents (with the exception of Vaccine Damage – see below). It is not enough to show that certain tablets or surgical treatment caused or contributed to your disability – you have to show that the tablets were negligently issued or the surgery negligently carried out. Because this can be quite complicated you will need the services of a good legal adviser. Start by contacting Action for Victims of Medical Accidents at 1 London Road, London SE23 3TP (tel: 01 291 2793). They will direct you to specialist solicitors in your area.

If you were disabled as a result of the effects of a vaccine, you may be able to claim Vaccine Damage compensation. Under this scheme you will be paid a tax-free lump sum if you were severely disabled as a result of a routine vaccination against one of the prescribed diseases. The vaccine may have been given to you, or to your mother when she was pregnant with you or (in the case of polio) to a person you look after from whom you contracted the disease. You do not have to prove anyone was at fault but you must be at least 80% disabled (for the assessment of percentages see pages 27–8). There are also other detailed conditions, for example about the place of vaccination and your age at the time. Write to the Vaccine Damage Payment Unit at North Fylde Central Office, Norcross, Blackpool FY5 3TA and ask for free leaflet HB3 *Payment for People Severely Disabled by a Vaccine.* It costs nothing to make a claim but you must act promptly. This time limit runs out six years from the date of vaccination (or, for a person vaccinated under the age of two, six years from their second birthday).

If I was injured in military service, can I claim compensation?

If you were injured during service in HM forces or during time of war you will be entitled to some compensation from the War Pensions Scheme. This covers people disabled by service between 1914 and 1921 or after 2 September 1939. (Those disabled between 1 October 1921 and 2 September 1939 should apply direct to the Ministry of Defence.) The basic compensation paid is a war disablement pension. This is awarded as a lump sum for disablement of less than 20% severity (see pages 27–8 for the assessment of percentages) and as a weekly pension in other cases. Both payments are tax-free but cannot be claimed while you are still in HM forces. In addition to the basic war disablement pension there are a range of additional allowances to compensate for lowered earnings, costs of additional clothing, cost of caring services etc. For an outline of the scheme, get the free leaflet FB 16 *Sick or Injured through Service in the Armed Forces* from your local main post office or local social security office. Leaflet FB 16 includes an order form for all other war pensioners' benefits leaflets. You make a claim by writing to War Pensions branch, DSS, Norcross, Blackpool FY5 3TA. There is no time limit within which you must make your claim but the sooner you claim the sooner you start being paid your war disablement pension.

If you have any difficulty with your claim or want to discuss the general help available to ex-service disabled people, contact your own ex-service organization or the local office of the War Pensioners Welfare Service (the address of the nearest branch can be found in Leaflet MPL 153 *Guide for the War Disabled* from the Leaflets Unit (address in Chapter 11).

If you were injured while serving in the forces but as a result of some negligence on the part of your superiors or colleagues rather than enemy action (for example, someone let go of your rope while you were on a training exercise) you could make a claim for compensation against the Ministry of Defence. You can only do this if the accident happened on or after 8 December 1986. Before that date the Ministry of Defence had 'crown immunity' and could not be sued. The first paragraphs of this chapter explain how to make a compensation claim.

If I was a civilian injured during the Second World War, can I claim compensation?

If you were a civilian or a Civil Defence worker and you are disabled as a result of the 1939–1945 war, you can claim compensation under the War Pensions Scheme in the same way as military personnel (although certain of the special allowances will not be paid) – see above.

If you were a merchant seafarer and disabled as a result of wounding or disease in time of war or are disabled due to the effects of detention by the enemy you can also claim under the War Pensions Scheme (see above).

If I am HIV positive as a result of a blood transfusion, can I claim compensation?

If you are a haemophiliac and HIV positive as a result of a contaminated blood transfusion you can claim financial help from the MacFarlane Trust established by the Government. Payments are discretionary and based on need. They are not intended to compensate for the fact of injected infection itself, rather to help you meet the costs of coping with the disability. You can get an application form by applying in writing to the MacFarlane Trust, PO Box 467, London SE1 7HU. Any payment you receive will not affect your social security benefits such as income support (page 80), family credit (page 79) or housing benefit (page 88).

It might also be possible to obtain compensation by claiming against the hospital authorities or the Department of Health for treating you with contaminated blood. At the time of writing several claims are under way. For the latest developments contact the Haemophilia Society at 123 Westminster Bridge Road, London SE1 7HR (tel: 01 928 2020).

If my child is severely disabled, can I claim compensation?

If you believe that the disability is someone's fault you should make a claim on behalf of your child for compensation in the normal way (see the opening paragraphs of this chapter).

Also, you may qualify for special help from the *Family Fund.* This is a trust fund which distributes money paid in by the Government. It is there to help families with severely disabled children meet some of the expenses of caring and to ease pressures. There is no limit to what you might claim help for, so you should apply for whatever you need. It might be the costs of a holiday for the family, or car hire to help with transportation or anything else which might help you to cope. It costs nothing to apply and you get the application form from the Family Fund, PO Box 50, York YO1 1UY. If you put in an application, the Fund will arrange for one of their qualified staff to visit you and discuss your request in greater detail. If you are not satisfied you can re-apply and appeal to the Management Committee if again refused.

In Chapter 6 there is more useful information on help available if you have a disabled child.

2. Employment

A. GETTING A JOB

What help can I get in finding a job?

If you are thinking about working for an employer (whether full or part time) there is plenty of information and advice to help you find and keep a job (see page 19 if you want to be self-employed). Although you could start job hunting by looking in newspapers or calling at employment agencies you will find that the local Job Centre can offer help with employment and training that is specifically suited to your needs. You can find the telephone number and address in the phone book under Department of Employment. (This is the Government Department which runs the Job Centres through its Employment Service.)

Job Centres offer help and advice free of charge. You can telephone or visit. If you feel that your disability is relevant to your employment prospects you should ask to speak to the Disablement Resettlement Officer (DRO). You will probably be invited to meet the Officer to discuss your specific interests and the help the Job Centre can offer.

The Disablement Resettlement Officer will outline the schemes available for training or help in getting or keeping a job. Many of these schemes are described below in summary form and you might find it useful to read through to the end of this chapter before you visit the Job Centre.

The DRO will also invite you to register with the Employment Service as a disabled person.

How do I register as disabled?

It is your choice whether or not you register as disabled with the Employment Service – the register is totally voluntary. However, although most of the usual services provided through the Job Centre and Government schemes are available whether you register or not, there are some which are restricted to those who are registered disabled. Also you might find that being registered is an advantage once you begin to seek work (see below).

The procedure is straightforward and is outlined in leaflet PWD5 *Disabled Persons Register* available free from any Job Centre. You get the application form from the Job Centre to complete and return to them. (School-leavers can get the form from the Careers Service.) They may ask you to have a medical certificate (which they will give you) completed by your own doctor. The GP should do this without payment. If your GP insists on making a charge and you do not wish to pay, return to the Job Centre and they will make alternative arrangements for you to be medically examined free of charge (any travel costs or loss of earnings will be met). If you are already registered as a *blind* person with social services you will probably not be asked to supply any other medical evidence.

You will be registered if you have already been disabled for a year (or you are likely to be disabled for 12 months or more). The formal requirements are that 'on account of injury, disease or congenital deformity' you are 'substantially handicapped in obtaining or keeping employment . . . of a kind which apart from that injury, disease or deformity would be suited' to your age, experience and qualifications.

If you are accepted on to the Register you will be issued with a Certificate of Registration known as a 'Green Card', valid for a fixed period. You will be invited to renew it before it expires.

If the DRO refuses your application for registration there is a procedure for review and you should take advice from one of the organizations mentioned in Chapter 11.

What training opportunities are available?

Most of the major Government training schemes, such as the new Employment Training Scheme (ETS) and the Youth Training Scheme (YTS), have places available for disabled people as well as the able-bodied. They are also run by the Department of Employment (in place of the Training Commission, formerly the Manpower Services Commission).

You can get a good idea what the schemes offer from the booklet *Your Guide to our Employment, Training & Enterprise Programmes* (leaflet PL856), available free from the Job Centre or main post offices. This leaflet is also available in languages other than English. Or you can get details of training opportunities from the Employment Department on 0800 24 6000 (your call is free).

Applications for courses are handled through the Job Centre, and the Disablement Resettlement Officer may be able to advise on the option most suitable to your needs. For many of the training programmes the conditions are modified and extra help may be available for the disabled.

Most schemes pay training allowances and generally this should provide a higher overall income than social security benefits alone.

What special training is available for a disabled person?

Training specifically for disabled people is available both on courses and in job placements.

Through the Job Centre you can get information about courses at Employment Rehabilitation Centres. There are 27 of these centres around the country, specially geared to meet the needs of disabled people. There you will be advised on the type of work or training best suited to your skills and placed on a course involving practical work experience to help you gain confidence and working capacity. If there is no Centre near you, the Job Centre will put you in touch with a more local work assessment scheme.

The courses offered are available free of charge and while attending you will be paid a tax-free allowance.

When you finish your course you might be offered the chance of a trial job with an employer for a further three weeks during which time your training allowance will continue. After that the employer might offer to take you on.

Can I get help with travel costs for interviews with employers or in looking for work?

Yes. The Job Centre will give you details of the financial help available through the *Travel to Interview Scheme*. You can only qualify if you apply before the interview takes place so it is a good idea to read the *Travel to Interview Handbook* (which sets out all the detailed conditions) at the Job Centre when you first start looking for work so that you will know what to do if you are offered interviews.

If you need to travel to different parts of the country to look for work you should ask about financial help under the *Job Search* scheme which is also administered from Job Centres.

Is there any help with travel costs once I start work?

If you can travel to work by public transport, see Chapter 7 (Travel & Leisure) on ways of reducing your travel costs.

If, however, because of your disability you have to use

other more expensive means of travel to work, and you are registered as disabled with the Employment Service (see above), you can get financial help with the cost. For example, you can get help with the cost of taxis to and from work if necessary. Ask at the local Job Centre for the details.

There is a weekly maximum to the amount of financial help available and this will be reduced if you receive a mobility allowance. You may not be eligible if you receive mobility allowance and could drive to work in your own car.

What is the Job Introduction Scheme?

This is a scheme under which employers are encouraged to offer employment opportunities to disabled people. In return for each job offered they are paid a weekly subsidy for the first six weeks worked by a newly employed disabled person.

If you or the Disablement Resettlement Officer find a job for which you both agree you are capable, the DRO could introduce you to the employer under the *Job Introduction Scheme.* If you are offered the job you will be paid the usual rate and the Employment Service will pay the subsidy direct to the employer.

The idea is that the six weeks will allow you to demonstrate your abilities and capabilities to the new employer who will then want to keep you on.

What if my disability means I need special tools or equipment for my job?

The Employment Service can supply on free loan any aid or adaptation necessary to help you do your job properly. This help is only available if you are registered as disabled with the Employment Service and you apply at the Job Centre.

The scheme is not confined to special equipment

designed for disabled people such as talking calculators or braille measuring devices. You can also get straight-forward items like tape recorders or adjustable stools and chairs. When you no longer need the item you simply return it.

Your employer could also get help with the cost of any adaptations necessary at the workplace to allow you to do your job fully. Grants of up to £6000 are available for each adaptation, e.g. the cost of installing a wheelchair ramp or the modification of machinery.

If you are *blind* and would find it helpful in your job to have someone to read for you, ask about the *Personal Reader Service* at the Job Centre. The scheme, which is run by the RNIB, is intended to help blind or partially sighted people to develop their careers or adjust to recent disability.

What if I'm not sure if I could manage in an ordinary working environment?

If you would prefer to work in an environment more sheltered than the open workplaces of non-disabled employees there will still be opportunities to find work. The Disablement Resettlement Officer will be able to tell you about Sheltered Workshops run by the local council or by a company called Remploy or by voluntary organ-izations. Here you can find work alongside other disabled colleagues.

An alternative is the *Sheltered Placement Scheme*. Under this scheme the Disablement Resettlement Officer arranges placements in open workplaces. You will work alongside non-disabled workers doing the same sorts of work but you will not be expected to achieve the same level of output and will be shielded from some of the other workplace pressures. You must be registered as disabled with the Employment Service in order to qualify.

What opportunities are there for long-term employment?

Obviously the Job Centre will have details of full and part-time jobs in your area but also information about other employment opportunities. In particular the Employment Service offers a number of employment schemes as well as training programmes.

If you are interested in self-employment ask for details of the *Enterprise Allowance Scheme.* This pays a weekly allowance for your first year in your own business if you can find a lump sum yourself to invest. There are also arrangements under which loans to get started in business can be underwritten (the *Loan Guarantee Scheme*) and encouragement given for investment in your business (*Business Expansion Scheme*). Training and information are available from the *Small Firms Service* which you can contact by telephoning 100 and asking for *Freephone Enterprise.*

If you are looking for paid work as an employee but are not successful in your first six months you should ask at the Job Centre about a *Job Club.* Your fares to the Job Club will be paid and, once there, you get free access to telephones, newspapers, stationery, etc. to help with your search for work. You will also be eligible for full or part-time work under any remaining local *Community Programme Scheme* which provides up to a year of work on a local project.

Everyone who has been looking for work for more than 6 months is invited for an interview with a Restart Officer who can offer help and advice on employment opportunities. But if you are seriously looking for work you do not need to wait before asking for a full interview with Job Centre staff to discuss employment opportunities. The leaflet *Your Guide to Employment, Training & Enterprise* (PL 856) available from your nearest main post office, gives a summary of all the schemes available.

Am I entitled to priority consideration by a prospective employer?

In practice many disabled people experience discrimination from employers in their search for work. But there are plenty of factors which should encourage a prospective employer to give your application priority:

(a) every employer with 20 or more staff has a legal duty to employ a percentage of registered disabled people among the workforce. This 'quota' is presently 3%. Although many are in breach of their obligations, a reasonable employer may positively be interested in recruiting you to help bring them up to the quota. If the employer is below the quota and you are qualified for a job vacancy a law passed in 1944 says that you must be offered the job unless the employer has obtained an exemption permit from the Department of Employment. If you think that the employer is not employing the appropriate number of disabled people and you don't get the job applied for, take advice from one of the agencies mentioned in Chapter 11.

(b) all large companies (250 or more staff) are obliged to disclose in their annual reports the steps they have taken to recognize the needs of disabled people in their workforce. They may be interested in recruiting disabled staff to help them appear to be positive in their approach to their responsibilities towards the disabled.

(c) various employment schemes and financial incentives (such as the Job Introduction Scheme described above) are encouraging employers to make more jobs available to the disabled, and the former Manpower Services Commission published a code of practice to help employers improve their treatment of the disabled (now available from the Employment Service, OP 57, 123 West St, Sheffield. S1 4ER).

These factors or a combination of them might help tip the balance in your favour in competing with an equally qualified able-bodied person.

It is now illegal for the employer to offer a disabled person lower wages or poorer conditions than would be offered to non-disabled staff.

B. AT WORK

If my disability means that I am finding it more difficult to cope at work, is any extra help available?

If you have not done so already, you should consider registering as disabled with the Employment Service (see above). Once registered, you will be entitled to join a scheme under which you can be loaned aids or equipment designed to make it easier for you to cope with your work (see above). The Disablement Resettlement Officer at the Job Centre should be able to advise about these steps and other assistance available.

The Disablement Advisory Service Manager (also at the Job Centre) could help by speaking to your employer about grant-aid for adaptations or new equipment in your work environment if that would assist you in your job. You may find it helpful to speak to your workplace representative if you are in a trade union. He or she may be able to suggest additional help available.

If you are not in a union, you could directly approach your employer or personnel officer to discuss your difficulties. He or she may be able to agree to transfer you to other lighter duties or could modify your job responsibilities or hours of work. Although they could suggest that you resign you do have some protection against dismissal (see below).

What if my disability is putting my job at risk?

Most employers are understanding about the need to have

time off work or to work more slowly on account of an illness or disability. In fact your contract of employment probably specifically deals with the amount of leave that is permitted and questions of sick pay, etc. However, if your ability to do your job is seriously affected by your illness or disability your employer might consider transferring you to other duties or even dismissing you.

If you are in a trade union, ask your local representative for help and advice. If the union is recognized by the employer there will probably be an agreed procedure for resolving any disputes about your job with the help of your union representative. If not, the union could simply take up your case directly with the employer.

If you are not in a union, contact one of the agencies mentioned in Chapter 11 for help and advice. The laws about employment rights are very complex and constantly changing and are not therefore set out in this book but an advice agency will know them and be able to help you in your dealings with the employer. You will also find information on your rights in *The Employees Handbook*, available in this series.

Should I accept an offer of 'early' or 'ill-health' retirement?

If your employer offers ill-health or early retirement (or there is a scheme at your workplace under which you could apply) you will have to weigh up all the relevant circumstances. Even if you are keen to carry on working full or part-time you might find it difficult to get other work if you left your present employment. You will also need to look at the way tax and social security rules will affect any payments your employer is intending to make to you as part of the retirement package. If you are approaching the end of your working life you will also want to consider the effect on any pension arrangements.

You must also consider what regular income you will

rely on once you leave work. If you are capable of work, you may well be refused unemployment benefit for as much as six months as a penalty for leaving your last job voluntarily (unless you had good reason for doing so). Any income support (see page 80) might be reduced, either for the same reason or because of the effect of any lump sum you receive from your employer.

Try and get your employer to give you all the details of the package being suggested (any lump sum, notice payment, reduced pension etc.) and then take some advice before you decide whether to accept. If you are in a trade union discuss the matter with your workplace representative. Otherwise consult one of the agencies mentioned in Chapter 11.

What if I am sacked because of my disability?

If you are dismissed by your employer and you believe your dismissal was unfair you may be able to claim compensation and even reinstatement. You need to act promptly in starting a claim for unfair dismissal. The procedures involved take several months so, in the meantime, you should claim unemployment benefit and income support (see Chapter 4) until you find another job.

Whether or not you can claim for unfair dismissal will depend on whether you worked full or part-time and how long you had been in your job. An advice agency or solicitor (see Chapter 11) can advise you about the possibilities of claiming compensation and help you bring your case before an Industrial Tribunal which deals with compensation claims.

In order to persuade the tribunal that your dismissal was fair the employer must show that he had a good reason for dismissing you and that he went about it in a reasonable way.

In your case the employer will probably say that the reason for dismissal was that you were no longer 'capable' of doing your job properly. But, even if the employer can prove that, it must also be shown that he or she acted reasonably in dismissing you. Your case will be much stronger if the employer failed to make proper inquiries about your personal circumstances and medical condition or failed to consider the possibility of redeployment to another job. The Industrial Tribunal will look at all the facts before deciding whether or not your dismissal was fair. You stand a far better chance of winning if you are represented when your case is heard. Your trade union or one of the agencies mentioned in Chapter 11 may be able to arrange representation for you free of charge.

What if I am sacked for some other reason, such as redundancy?

In your case, if you are eligible to bring a claim of unfair dismissal (see above), the employer will need to show that not only was a fair and reasonable procedure followed in selecting staff for redundancy but that as part of 'acting reasonably' he or she took specific account of your disability before taking the decision to dismiss you.

This is all the more important if you are registered disabled with the Employment Service because under laws passed in 1944 an employer cannot sack a registered disabled person without 'reasonable cause' if this would leave disabled workers less than 3% of the workforce.

In one case in 1985 a company facing a redundancy situation asked all employees to take the same capability test. The disabled employee's result was assessed as being in the mid-band. Later, all the staff in the lower and mid-bands were made redundant without further inquiry. The Employment Appeal Tribunal ruled that this would mean the disabled person had been unfairly dismissed unless the employers could prove that they had considered his specific circumstances and disability before simply including him in the group to be dismissed.

If my disability was caused by an injury at work, what should I do to claim compensation?

The first thing to do is report the injury to your employer and make sure that it is recorded in the accident book (any employer with ten or more staff must have one). If you work for a very small firm it might be worth writing a note of your injury and having the employer sign it so you have a written record. You should make sure every type of injury is recorded. Even something apparently minor can develop into a serious disability later. To ensure that you can later get appropriate compensation you can apply to the social security office for a declaration that you have had an industrial accident. Ask for form BI 95 at a social security office.

Next you need to make sure you have an income to live on while you go about claiming compensation. If you are able to carry on working in spite of your injury, and are happy to do so, your wages or salary will see you through. If you are off work because of the injury, check your contract of employment for details of any sick pay and sick leave to which you are entitled. If you don't have a copy of your contract (or you were never issued with a written one) ask your employer or personnel officer about sick leave and sick pay.

If your injury makes you incapable of work you will normally be paid statutory sick pay by your employer for up to 28 weeks absence from work (for all the details about statutory sick pay see page 94).

Once you have taken care of your immediate income needs you should consider claiming compensation for your injury. The two main ways of getting compensation are described in outline later in this chapter but you will probably find it helpful to take some detailed advice at an early stage. If you are in a trade union contact your local representative as soon as possible. Most unions have very good arrangements for helping members injured at work.

This will certainly cover expert and legal advice but might also entitle you to some cash help from union funds. If your local representative does not prove particularly helpful don't give up. Write to the regional office or the head office of the union and ask for help to take up your case.

There are two broad types of compensation available for people injured at work: the state-run Industrial Injuries Scheme and the private compensation arrangements. You should consider claiming compensation under both.

What is the Industrial Injuries Scheme?

This is the national Government scheme to provide compensation to people who are injured at work or who are affected by a work-related disease. If you work for an employer you are automatically a member (if you were injured while self-employed see below). The scheme covers any injury you suffer arising out of your work or during the course of your work. This means not only something directly related to your job (e.g. a back injury caused by the lifting required in your work) but also other injuries at work (for example, tripping up in the corridor on your way to your desk).

The scheme provides cash help by way of specific benefits. These are not means-tested and you do not need to have paid National Insurance contributions but they all have detailed conditions. You claim the benefits from your local social security office and the whole process is free of charge. If you think that you might be entitled, put in a claim. The main benefits are:

Non-contributory Sickness and Injury Benefit

If your injury has made you incapable of work you would normally claim statutory sick pay (SSP) from your employer (see above). If for some reason SSP is not payable (for example because you were on a very low wage) you will be paid sickness benefit by DSS instead. Your employer should give you a form on which to make your claim. If you are still incapable of work after six months you will be paid invalidity benefit which is worth much more. Normally you can only be eligible for sickness and invalidity benefits if you have paid sufficient National Insurance contributions but because you were injured at work those rules are not applied to you.

Disablement Benefit

Whether or not you can carry on working you can get compensation for any accident at work which causes a serious loss of physical or mental faculty. To qualify, the 'loss of faculty' must represent a disablement of not less than 14% compared to a fully able-bodied person (see below for how the assessment is made). This loss of faculty may result from more than one accident. So if you suffer two minor injuries (perhaps in different accidents) each resulting in 7% disablement, the total of 14% will qualify you for disablement benefit.

You will receive a weekly disablement benefit payable on top of any other National Insurance benefit or earnings. The amount increases according to the extent of your disablement up to a maximum at 100% disablement. The procedure for claiming is straightforward. All the details are in social security Leaflet NI 6 *Industrial Injuries Disablement Benefit* which you can get free from your local social security office together with a claim form (BI 100A). There are separate leaflets and claim forms available for different types of industrial diseases, occupational deafness, pneumoconiosis, byssinosis, etc.

There are time limits for claiming disablement benefit so do not delay in getting and completing the forms. Your entitlement starts 15 weeks after the industrial accident. If you claim late you should ask for backdating to the start of your entitlement. If refused, seek advice from one of the places mentioned in Chapter 11.

The staff at the local DSS office make the basic decisions on your claim (such as whether you suffered an industrial accident) and then refer your case to a medical specialist for decision. The medical specialists (called adjudicating medical authorities) will decide if you have suffered a loss of faculty causing disablement and will assess the percentage for that disablement. Loss of all sight or hearing would qualify for 100% disablement. Less serious injuries attract a lower percentage. You will be medically examined and a *final* assessment will be made if your disablement will last for life or for a specific fixed period. If the authorities are unsure about how your disablement will develop you will be given a *provisional* assessment and examined again later. If you disagree with the assessment you have three months in which to appeal to a Medical Appeal Tribunal. The agencies mentioned in Chapter 11 or your trade union might be able to provide representation. If your disablement gets worse than expected or you get some fresh evidence of the serious-ness of your condition your percentage can be reassessed later by asking for a review.

Reduced Earnings Allowance

This benefit is paid to compensate you for lost earnings if you are unable to return to your usual job or an equiva-lent one because of the effects of an accident at work. It is quite separate from disablement benefit and can be paid on top of that benefit or any earnings or on its own. The amount paid is set by looking at the difference between what you can now earn and what you would be earning had you not had the accident. The benefit is paid weekly up to a prescribed maximum amount. You claim on form BI 103, available from your social security office. The main condition is that you must have suffered a disablement which has been (or could be) assessed at between 1 and 100% and you are not able to attract the same level of earnings as before the accident.

Other Benefits

Two special allowances are available to people claiming disablement benefit. *Constant attendance allowance* is available to those with assessments totalling 100% disablement who need regular care or attention on account of the disability – for example people who are blind, deaf, confined to bed or paralysed. The allowance is paid as a regular weekly sum at one of four different rates. Claim on form BI 104 from the local DSS office.

If you are receiving the higher rates of constant attendance allowance and your need for assistance is likely to be permanent you will be paid an additional *exceptionally severe disablement allowance*.

How do I claim compensation from my employer for an accident at work?

If your accident was in some way the responsibility of your employers you may well be able to claim compensation against them. All employers have to take out insurance against this possibility and must display the insurance certificate at the workplace to show that this has been done.

You could simply ask your employer for compensation yourself but your claim is likely to be taken much more seriously if it is made by an adviser on your behalf.

If you are in a trade union, the union probably employs industrial compensation specialists. If not, they will certainly have solicitors able to handle such claims and the union will normally pay any costs involved. Ask your union representative.

If you are not in a union the best way forward is to consult a solicitor. Under the Accident Legal Advice Service (ALAS) you can have a half hour free consultation with a solicitor to discuss your prospects for claiming compensation. To find a solicitor who is in the ALAS scheme contact your local Citizens' Advice Bureau for names and addresses (or phone 01 242 2430). If the solicitor advises that you have a claim she or he will also advise you as to the necessary steps to take and the possibility of getting legal aid to meet any legal fees.

You don't have to be sure that your accident was the employer's fault before you seek advice. You might even be able to get compensation if the accident was caused by colleagues at work or by a contractor working with your employer. If in doubt, take advice. Whatever you do, don't delay. There is a fixed period within which you must make your claim for compensation (usually three years from the date of the accident).

What if I was self-employed when I was injured?
Hopefully you took out insurance against personal injury when you started your business and, if so, you should make a claim for compensation under your insurance policy.

If someone else was to blame for the injury you received you should consider claiming compensation from them. Take advice about it from one of the agencies mentioned in Chapter 11. Alternatively, make an appointment for a free interview with a solicitor under the Accident Legal Advice Scheme. Your local Citizens' Advice Bureau has the details. If you are unable to work as a result of the accident, claim sickness benefit from the local social security office. Whether you receive benefit will depend on your National Insurance contributions record.

Whether or not you receive sickness benefit, you may also be eligible for income support or housing benefit (see Chapter 4).

If you were only 'nominally' self-employed (for

example your employer insisted on it for tax and National
Insurance purposes) but you were really an employee
when you were injured, you should take advice from one
of the agencies mentioned in Chapter 11 because you
might qualify for help under the Industrial Injuries
Scheme described on pages 26–9.

3. Housing

What assistance can I get with my housing needs?
As a disabled person you might be seeking help with housing for two main reasons. Either you have a home but need help in coping with some aspect of it or you have no satisfactory home (either because you have no home at all or the one you have is unsuitable as a result of your disability). In this chapter both these problems are considered by looking at each of the possible situations in turn. First we look at people who have homes (as owner-occupiers, private tenants, housing association tenants or council tenants) and then at people who are seeking housing or alternative homes. Look at the section which best applies to you.

A. YOUR PRESENT HOME

1. Owner-Occupiers

Is there any help available with the costs of paying for my home?
Various forms of financial help are available to home owners, especially those who have a mortgage or secured loan from a bank or building society:

(a) *tax relief* is currently allowed on borrowing of up to £30,000 for house purchase or home improvement on your own home. In practice, this means the lender will usually only ask you for payments net of tax rather than the full amount.

(b) if you are claiming income support (see Chapter 4), the social security office will pay at least half (and in most circumstances the whole) of the interest part of any mortgage or homeloan repayments.

Neither of these forms of assistance are especially more generous to you because you are disabled but you may find it helpful to read *The Owner-Occupiers Handbook*, available in this series, which is full of information on meeting the costs associated with home ownership.

The golden rule if you have financial problems with your housing costs is to let your lender know as soon as possible. A responsible lender will be able to suggest modifications to your loan or the rate of repayments if these are necessary and will take full account of the effect of your disability on your ability to repay. You can also get general advice and information about any problems meeting housing costs from *Housing Debtline* (see Chapter 11 for details).

Can I get help with the costs of necessary repairs or improvements?

There are five ways of getting financial help with the costs of any repairs and improvements that your home needs. You can try any one or a combination of them:

(a) you could *borrow* the necessary money from a building society, bank or other responsible lender. You will usually be asked to agree to your home being used to secure the loan (ultimately this means that if you fail to pay, the lender could sell your home to get the money back) and you will have to show that you have sufficient income to make repayments. The loan will therefore be made either by way of increasing the mortgage of your home or by a second or further 'mortgage'. If you are claiming income support (see Chapter 4) you can get help with paying the interest charged on a loan taken out for repairs and improvements, and possibly a Social Fund grant to cover the legal and survey fees (see below).

(b) you could apply for a *grant* from the local housing

authority (usually the local District or Borough Council). Whether you get a grant and how much help you are awarded will depend on the age of your house, the type of work required and your financial circumstances but it might amount to as much as 90% of the costs. This book does not set out the different types of grant available as these were under review at the time of writing. For up to date details get the Government leaflet *Paying for Repairs and Improvements to Your Home* from your local Citizens Advice Bureau or see *The Owner-Occupiers Handbook*, available in this series. Then ask your local council for information about the grant aid available locally and about any extra help they give to disabled applicants. (The grant will not meet all of the costs so you will have to put in some money yourself – but see below if the work is necessary because of your disability.) If you are going to apply for a grant do not start any of the repair or improvement work until you receive the official outcome of your application or you may lose the grant altogether.

(c) you can apply to the social services department of your local County or Metropolitan Borough Council (Regional Council in Scotland) for financial help. They have a duty to provide advice and assistance to the disabled. A specialist worker will visit and assess the need for the work you want done. They can authorize a grant to help you meet the costs or could contribute towards the cost if the balance will be paid by a house renovation grant (see above).

(d) if you are receiving income support (see Chapter 4) you could apply for a *grant* from the Social Fund. As a disabled person you would have priority in consideration for such a grant, especially if the repair or improvement means that you will be able to stay in your own home rather than having to move to a caring institution. The definitions of people eligible are very flexible and the officer has a wide discretion in making a grant. Normally these grants are only available for small improvements, repairs and decoration works. If you need a larger sum the Social Fund officer will probably suggest that you take out an ordinary loan from a lending institution (see above) and then repay with the help of income support. However, you can also get a Social Fund *grant* for the cost of the legal and survey fees involved in arranging that loan. Whatever sum you need, ask your local social security office to send you the form for a Social Fund community care grant (SF300).

(e) you might find that there is a 'Care & Repair' scheme operating in your neighbourhood. This offers advice to home owners about financial help with the costs of repairs and improvements and practical help in selecting builders and ordering the work. The Citizens Advice Bureau can put you in touch with any local Care and Repair scheme or an equivalent such as the 'Staying Put' scheme run by Anchor Housing Trust.

How can I get help with the costs of aids and adaptations necessary for my home as a result of my disability?

If you need to install new facilities or have adaptations made to your home as a result of your disability you should contact the Social Services Department of your County Council or Metropolitan Borough Council (Social Work Department of the Regional Councils in Scotland). A social services worker will arrange a visit to discuss your needs with you and help you with applications for any local authority housing grants (see above) that may be appropriate. They will be able to advise you as to any preferential arrangement available to the disabled. They may also have schemes for financial help with meeting the difference between the cost of the works and the normal renovation grants.

Before the visit you might find it helpful to read

Housing Grants and Allowances from the Royal Association for Disability and Rehabilitation (RADAR) (see Chapter 11 for the address) so that you have an idea of what may be available. See also *The Owner-Occupiers Handbook*, available in this series.

For aids and adaptations which are not structural (e.g. telephones) see Chapter 10.

Will I have to pay VAT on repair or improvement work?

Most ordinary building alterations attract VAT liability and you will have to pay VAT to the contractor.

However, where work is being carried out to make property more usable by a disabled person no VAT is levied (for example, to construct a wheelchair ramp or a downstairs lavatory).

To check whether you will be liable for VAT ask your contractor to tell you whether the estimate of the cost of the works excludes or includes VAT. Then call your local Customs and Excise Office (where VAT is collected) – the number is under 'C' in the phone book – and tell them the type of work you are having done. They will advise whether VAT should be charged.

What if my own home is no longer suitable for my needs?

If you own your own home you will probably first consider selling up to buy something more appropriate. However, very little property for sale is specifically designed and built to meet the needs of disabled people and you may have some difficulty finding exactly the right property for you.

An alternative would be to sell your own home to a housing association which specifically provides accommodation for the disabled. In return for your existing home they may be able to offer you suitably adapted housing association property. Contact your local council's Housing Department and ask for details of any association operating in this way in the area.

You are unlikely to find the sort of accommodation you need available in the *private* rented sector but some council housing or housing association property may be appropriate. It will be in great demand. Start by putting in an application to the Housing Department of your local council for rehousing and set out the type of accommodation you need (ground floor, centrally heated, etc., as appropriate). They cannot legally refuse to put you on the housing waiting list but once on the list you may well find that others are treated as being in more pressing need than you. If you find that your circumstances are not being fully considered, arrange to see your local District (or Borough) Councillor to get him or her involved on your behalf. The council could put your name forward to a specialist housing association operating in the area.

If you think you would prefer specially adapted or sheltered accommodation see below at pages 59–62.

If your circumstances are such that it is no longer reasonable to expect you to carry on living in your home, the local council could accept you as 'homeless' (see below, page 53). You could suggest this to them as it may get you more priority in receiving offers of other accommodation.

Can I get any help with paying the general rates?
There are three ways of getting help to pay your general rates (water rates are dealt with separately below).

(a) you could apply for a *rate rebate*. This is a type of housing benefit and is worked out by considering your income and savings along with the amount of rates you have to pay and the circumstances of any other people living in your home (Chapter 4 gives more details about all types of housing benefit including rate rebates). Most disabled home owners on modest incomes qualify for rate rebates because the scheme is slightly more generous to those who are disabled (or have disabled people living with them) than to able-bodied people.

The normal maximum rebate is 80% of your annual rates bill but if your needs are exceptional, for example because much of your income is spent meeting needs which flow from your disability, you can ask for rebate of up to 100%. You get the application form from the local council (details should also be included with the rates bill sent to you every year).

(b) you could apply for a *rate rebate on account of your disability.* These rebates are paid under a law passed in 1978 and are not part of the housing benefit scheme, so it does not matter what income or savings you have. You do not have to be registered as 'disabled' with the social services department. You will qualify if there is some facility or feature in your home which is 'essential or of major importance' to your well-being. The feature or facility does not have to be some special extra addition or adaptation you have made – it may have been present when you bought the property. The sort of facilities and features that count are: particular rooms (e.g. set aside for therapy or treatment connected with your disability), additional bathrooms or lavatories, extra floor space for a wheelchair, parking or garage facilities for a vehicle and heating systems in the house. The law lays down the amount of discount you are entitled to for the most common types of facility and in other cases the amount is assessed by a valuation officer. The council can agree to increase your rebate by another 20% on top of the fixed amounts and you should certainly ask for that extra help if you need it.

You claim the disabled persons rebate on a form available from the Rates Office which sent your rates bill and you can apply at any time in the year. If you realize that you could have applied for the relief in some previous rating year, ask for your claim to be backdated. If you are not already registered as disabled with a social services department (see page 128) you may be asked for some supporting information about your disabilities e.g. a letter from your GP. If you are refused a rebate or you think you are receiving too little there are rights of appeal. Take advice from one of the agencies mentioned in Chapter 11.

A free Government leaflet, *Rate Relief for Disabled Persons*, gives more details about the rebate scheme and is available from larger libraries and Citizens Advice Bureaux.

If you claim both housing benefit and the disabled person's rate rebate, the reduction in your rates on account of your disability will be made first and housing benefit will then be worked out on that lower figure.

(c) you can ask the Rating Authority to reduce your rates on account of any difficult financial circumstances. The law says that the council can reduce your rates (in part or altogether) on account of your 'poverty'. Not many people apply for this because in most situations the housing benefit rate rebate (see above) is available to meet rates for people on low incomes. But if you do not feel you are getting enough help from that scheme, or you do not qualify for it for some reason, you could apply for this straightforward rates reduction. There is no application form for the reduction and you may find the council very reluctant even to consider your case when you write to them. If you get an unhelpful reply, write back mentioning the law itself (section 53 General Rate Act 1967) or take some advice from one of the agencies mentioned in Chapter 11.

Can I get help with the community charge (or poll tax)?

The community charge replaces general rates in Scotland from April 1989 and in England and Wales from April 1990.

Most disabled people (and adult members of their families) will be due to pay the same amounts as the able-bodied. The conditions for exemption from the charge are described on page 101.

You can apply for a rebate on the community charge you are due to pay. The rebates are administered by the same authority that sends you the community charge you are receiving income support (see Chapter 4) you will receive 80% rebate. If you are not receiving income support the amount of rebate you receive will depend upon your savings, your income and your personal circumstances.

Again, as a disabled person you receive some limited preferential treatment when the calculations are made. The maximum rebate you can receive is 80% so that you will always have to find one-fifth of the community charge money yourself.

Where can I get more information about being an owner-occupier?
There is a separate *Owner-Occupiers Handbook* published in this series and soon to be available from bookshops and libraries.

2. Private Tenants

Can I get any financial help with my rent?
If you are on a modest income (whether from earnings or benefits) you are probably qualified to receive a rent allowance. This is a type of housing benefit which you can claim from your local housing authority (usually the District or Borough Council). How much you receive will depend on your income and savings, the amount of your rent, the way it is made up and the circumstances of any other people living in your home. The maximum is 100% of the rent you are liable to pay, so rent allowance is well

worth claiming. The council will either pay the money regularly to you to put towards the rent or, if you prefer (or if there are very bad arrears), they can pay the allowance direct to your landlord. Although all private tenants can apply for rent allowance the scheme is slightly more generous because you are disabled or have someone disabled living in your household.

If you have not already claimed rent allowance (and perhaps have run up some arrears) ask on your application form for the allowance to be backdated. The benefit authorities can backdate for up to one year. Also, if you feel that you need more help towards your rent than has been allowed you should ask for more. The benefit authorities can pay you extra allowance in 'exceptional circumstances'. Being in difficulties as a result of your disability will often be accepted as 'exceptional'.

Can I get any financial help with my rates?
If you pay rates, whether directly to the council or to your landlord, you can apply for all or any of the three types of rebates mentioned above for home owners (see pages 37–9).

Do I qualify for help towards paying the community charge (or poll tax)?
You can claim for a rebate or an exemption in exactly the same way as for owner-occupiers (see pages 39–40).

What rights do I have to stay in my home?
The law about your rights and your landlord's rights is quite complicated and you may well need to take advice about your particular circumstances from one of the agencies mentioned in Chapter 11. The golden rule is not to move out or agree to change your tenancy agreement until you have taken independent advice. For the full details you could consult *The Private Tenants Handbook* which is also available in this series.

Can I make improvements or adaptations which are necessary because of my disability?

If you are sure about your rights to stay in your home (see above), the first thing to consider is whether the improvements are the landlord's responsibility. For example, if your disability means it is now more necessary for your flat or house to have the *standard amenities* (a bath or shower, washbasin, sink, hot and cold water or inside WC) and these are not already available, you should ask your landlord to install them. The landlord will probably qualify for a grant to help pay for the cost. If you can't contact the landlord or the landlord fails to respond, write to the Chief Environmental Health Officer of your local council. That officer will arrange for you to be visited and will then require your landlord to carry out the necessary works to install standard amenities.

If your home already has these standard amenities but you want it improved to cater better for your disability (or that of a member of your family) you should discuss your needs with your landlord. You cannot insist that the work is done, but if the landlord declines you could ask for permission to do the work yourself. You will need this in writing. If your tenancy is fully protected under the Rent Act, the landlord cannot unreasonably refuse you permission to carry out improvements. If you are refused you must be given reasons in writing and you can challenge the refusal in court. The agencies listed in Chapter 11 can advise you on how to do this. Even if you are fully protected you should consider whether the best way forward is really to improve your landlord's property. In the long run you might be better off trying first to move to a suitably adapted council or housing association house or flat (see below under Finding a Home). If you are an *assured* tenant any rights you have to do improvement work will be set out in your tenancy agreement.

If you are not a fully protected tenant, it is probably

not worth doing the improvements anyway as your land-lord will be able to get a court order for possession of your home if he or she objects to the work you propose to do.

Once you have permission to go ahead (or your tenancy agreement specifically says that you have the right to do improvements) the next step will be financing the project. The various forms of financial help available are described above (see pages 33–6) in relation to owner-occupiers and all of them are equally available to private tenants. In particular, housing renovation grants are available and are more generous where the improvement work is necessary to meet the needs of a disabled occupier.

Will my rent be increased on account of any improvements or adaptations?

If you carry out the improvement works yourself your rent will not normally be affected, but before you start the work take advice from one of the agencies mentioned in Chapter 11.

If your landlord carries out the work, he or she may try to increase the rent. If you have a registered fair rent this can only be done by application to the Rent Officer. If the adaptations are necessary because of your circumstances you should object to them being taken into account for increasing the rent, as they are personal to you as occupier and do not generally increase the value of your home. However, if the improvements would benefit any tenant, the Rent Officer may well increase the rent. But any rent allowance you receive (see pages 40–41) should be increased to take account of your higher rent.

If you are an *assured* tenant it is very likely that your rent will be increased.

What if my rented home is no longer suitable for my needs?

You could try to find other more suitable accommodation in the private sector, either with your current landlord or with a different one. Your landlord may be prepared to offer you some financial incentive to move out of your current home. Take some advice from one of the agencies mentioned in Chapter 11.

An alternative would be to apply to a housing association which caters specifically for the needs of disabled people. You can find out which ones might be appropriate by contacting your local council Housing Department as they should know which associations operate in your area. Otherwise try one of the agencies mentioned in Chapter 11 for advice.

Another alternative which you might like to pursue at the same time would be to apply for council housing in the area where you want to live. They will probably have an application form (available from the Housing Department) and will assess your needs in considering you for any suitable tenancy. Not all councils have suitable properties for people with differing disabilities and those that do often have a long queue. But don't be put off. Send in your application and if you don't feel you are getting sufficient priority see your local councillor.

If it is no longer reasonable for you to go on living in your privately rented home the council could accept you as 'homeless'. You should mention this to the council as it may be a way of getting more priority in being offered other accommodation (see page 53).

Of course, if you have the financial resources and you can identify a suitable property, you could buy your own home.

Where can I get more information about my position as a private tenant?

There is a separate *Private Tenants Handbook* available in this series from bookshops and libraries.

3. Housing Association Tenants

What help can I get towards my rent?

If you have been living in housing association accommodation since before 1989 your rent is probably fixed by the independent Rent Officer. If you feel the registered rent is too high you could apply to have it reviewed or you might be able to appeal against the amount of rent set. Take advice from one of the agencies mentioned in Chapter 11.

If you have taken up housing association accommodation on or after 15 January 1989 you may have accepted an 'assured tenancy'. Under this arrangement the association and you will usually have agreed the initial rent and the tenancy agreement will set out how and when the rent can be raised and by what amounts. If you feel the rent is too high, check your tenancy agreement and, if dissatisfied, see your local housing association staff.

You can qualify for help towards paying the rent under the rent allowance scheme described for private tenants (see pages 40–41).

Is there any help with general rates or the community charge (poll tax)?

There are rebate schemes for both. You can qualify for help or exemption in the same way as described for home owners (pages 37–40).

What if my housing association home is no longer suitable or requires adaptations and improvements?

You should discuss your particular needs with the housing

association staff as soon as possible. They may be prepared to offer you a transfer to a more suitable property or could arrange an exchange with a different association which provides accommodation more geared to your needs. If the association cannot or will not help you find another home, you will have to make arrangements yourself (see page 44).

If you want to stay where you are, the association can arrange to carry out the necessary repairs and improvements to your home. The housing association will probably seek advice and financial help from the local council Housing Department and social services office. Staff of those organizations will visit you to discuss your requirements before the work starts.

You cannot force the association to do the work you require. If they are unwilling, you could arrange for the work to be done yourself. For details of how to go about this and the help available with the cost see the relevant details below given for council tenants. If you have an 'assured tenancy' see page 42.

Where can I get more information about my position as a housing association tenant?

The Public Tenants Handbook, available in this series from bookshops and libraries, deals with the position of housing association tenants.

4. Council Tenants

What help can I get with paying my rent?

Your council landlord can only charge a 'reasonable' rent. If you feel that your rent is unreasonably high for your home ask your local councillor to help you get a reassessment from the council. If this doesn't help, approach one of the agencies mentioned in Chapter 11.

If your rent is a reasonable one but you have financial difficulty in meeting it you would probably qualify for a rent rebate. This is a type of housing benefit (see page 88). The amount you are entitled to depends on your income and savings, the amount of your rent, the way it is made up and the circumstances of the other people living in your home. The calculation is more generous to disabled tenants and those with disabled partners or children than the able-bodied. The scheme is administered by the same council which is your landlord. You claim on a form which you can get free from the council's Rent Office or Housing Department. You can get as much as 100% of your rent paid depending upon your circumstances and the council will usually pay the rebate straight into your rent account.

If you have already run up some arrears ask the council to 'backdate' your claim (they can pay you up to a year's worth of back payments). Also the council has power to pay more rebate each week if your circumstances are exceptional. So make sure you mention any specific difficulties and your disability on the application form and ask for backdating or more rebates as you think appropriate.

What help can I get with general rates?
You can apply for a rate rebate in the same way as for a rent rebate (see above), to the same council and usually on the same application form. More details on rebates and the special help you are entitled to on account of your disabilities are on page 88.

What help can I get towards the community charge (or poll tax)?
Depending upon your income, savings and personal circumstances you may qualify for exemption or a rebate against the charge. The rules are the same as for owner-occupiers (see page 39 above).

Can I get the council to make necessary improvements to my home?

If, on account of your disability (or that of someone in your household), you feel that alterations or improvements to your home would be useful, contact the Housing Department of the council to discuss your needs.

You will probably be visited at home by a housing officer who will consider what is required. If he or she agrees that the adaptation would be practical, the Housing Department could carry out the work for you free of charge. Indeed, they have a legal obligation to consider the housing needs of disabled people. However, housing authorities have many pressures on the resources available to them and because they do not *have* to do the work you seek they may decline to do so. A local councillor may be able to press for more consideration on your behalf.

If the Housing Department cannot help, approach the social services department of the County or Regional Council (Borough Council in metropolitan areas). They do have a legal duty to assess your needs and to arrange for any necessary improvements to be made on account of disability.

The first step will be a visit from a member of the social services staff who will advise on the sort of help available and the length of any waiting list of other tenants due to receive this help.

An alternative would be to arrange the improvement work yourself. You can claim help with the financial costs involved through various housing renovation grants (see pages 33–5). You need to apply to the local council for the grant before you start work. The grant conditions are slightly more generous if you are disabled or have someone disabled living in your home.

As a council tenant you will need written permission from the council to carry out any improvement work. Permission cannot be unreasonably refused and if it is refused you have a right of appeal to a court. However, before starting work you should bear in mind that, although the improvement will not affect your rent, it will be to the benefit of your landlord's rather than your own property.

Where can I get more information about my position as a council tenant?

There is a separate *Public Tenants Handbook* available in this series from bookshops and libraries.

Can I insist on a transfer to other more suitable council accommodation?

You may well want to move to other council accommodation on account of your disability. Possibly you will want to move nearer to supportive friends or relatives or to accommodation on the ground floor or with central heating. Although you have no legal right to insist on a transfer, the law requires each council to keep a set of rules about arrangements for transfers in their area. You can ask to see the full rules at the council offices or you could ask for a free summary which the council is obliged to publish.

The rules (or the summary of them) should give you a good idea what prospects you have of successfully getting a transfer and the priority you will receive compared with others who wish to move. You should then ask your local Housing Office to send you the form (if there is one) or tell you whom you should write to about a transfer. You might find that you get extra priority if you are registered as disabled with social services (see page 129) and if you have the support of your GP or a social worker. If you feel that your application is not being dealt with according to the rules or that you have been given insufficient priority, go to see your local councillor. Your local library can give you the name and address.

If you want to move to a completely different council area you should ask about the *National Mobility Scheme* at your local Housing Department Office. They will provide you with a leaflet about the scheme and an application form. If your local council accept your application they will forward it to your chosen council for them to consider whether you can move to that area.

B. FINDING A HOME

How can I go about finding a home if I don't already have one or my present home is unsuitable?
The rest of this chapter describes the ways in which you can get a home with the help of the local council in the area where you want to live. Of course, you could also pursue the alternatives of buying a home of your own or renting from a private landlord or a housing association. The financial and other help available to owner-occupiers and private tenants is described in earlier parts of this chapter and if you are thinking of making private arrangements you should read there.

This chapter also considers what you should do if you want to move to residential accommodation specifically designed to care for your needs, for example, a private or council care home for older disabled people.

Whom should I approach first?
Your first approach should be to the Housing Department of the local authority for the area where you want to live. Usually this will be the District or Borough Council. They may want you to complete an application form for accommodation or they might arrange an interview with you either at your present address or at the council offices. As an added alternative you could ask them if there are any

housing associations operating in the area where you want to live which might also have accommodation suited to your needs.

If your need for a home arises in an emergency (e.g. you are about to be discharged from hospital or your previous home has been damaged or destroyed) ask to speak to the person handling 'Emergency Homeless' applications. If the need arises outside office hours, the council may run a telephone emergency service on the town hall number or you should go to your local police station where they will have details of emergency social service arrangements.

How will the council deal with my application for accommodation?

The council has a legal duty to consider your application in one of three ways. It is either dealt with as a *routine application* for council accommodation or as an application under the procedures for '*homeless persons*' or as an application under the *National Assistance Act*. The next few pages outline the main differences between the way these three types of procedure operate. Read through to identify the one which most applies to you and check that it is the one the council is operating. If you find it is not, tell the council officers dealing with your application. If still dissatisfied, seek advice from one of the agencies listed in Chapter 11.

You should also complain if you feel the council is being slow in dealing with your application.

What is the procedure for a 'routine' application for housing?

Every council is required by law to keep a set of rules about how it allocates its flats and houses to people who apply for council housing, and a similar set of rules about the procedures it follows in choosing the new tenants.

You can see a set of the rules at the town hall. You can even buy a copy and you are entitled (free of charge) to a summary of those rules. A look at the rules (or the summary) should indicate what prospects you have of being offered a home by the council.

It is up to each council to decide how to select tenants. The council you apply to might have a date-order scheme (under which allocations depend on how long you have been on the list) or a points scheme (where priority in the form of points is given for various housing needs) or a merits scheme (where each case is looked at individually, perhaps by councillors) or a combination of these schemes. The rules will tell you which one is operating for that area.

By law the council must consider your application in accordance with its scheme. It can't just rule you out because you don't already live in the area, or you have a home somewhere else.

Whether you get council accommodation depends on how much property is available and what priority you have compared to other applicants. The law does require that you be given some preference if you have a large family, or your present home is overcrowded, insanitary or in poor condition, or you are being dealt with as homeless (see below).

There is a legal requirement that the authority must recognize the special needs of the disabled and you should therefore find that your application will be given priority because you are disabled.

You may find that once your application has been assessed you are simply placed on a 'waiting list' along with many other people. You should check that your application has been properly assessed in accordance with the rules. If you feel that you should check that your see if a GP or social worker will write to the council in support of your application.

If the 'routine procedure' offers no reasonable prospect of housing in the near future, consider one of the other two procedures described below.

What is the 'homeless persons' procedure?

The law requires local councils to give special attention to people who apply for accommodation and may be homeless. As is explained below, you do not have to be 'on the streets' to be helped under this procedure. To make sure that you get help this way ask to be dealt with under Part 3 of the Housing Act 1985.

The first thing that the law requires is that the council make inquiries into your application. Whether you will receive housing (and/or housing advice) from the council depends on what they discover about whether you are homeless, whether you are in priority need and whether you are homeless intentionally.

The full details of your legal rights under this procedure are set out in *The Homeless Persons Handbook* in this series and now available from libraries and bookshops. This chapter can offer only the briefest summary of those rights.

Am I a 'homeless person'?

The law says that the council must accept you as homeless if you have no accommodation in England, Scotland or Wales.

Not all accommodation counts. Even if you already have somewhere to stay you will be treated as homeless unless all three of the following conditions are fulfilled:

(a) you have a legal right to occupy or the real owner cannot evict you without a court order *and*

(b) it is big enough to accommodate you and the people you live with *and*

(c) it is reasonable for you to carry on living there

Even if these three conditions are satisfied in your case

you will still be accepted as homeless if you can't get into your accommodation (e.g. because you have been locked out) or staying there would lead to violence (or threats of violence from some other resident). You are also homeless if you have a 'mobile' home and nowhere to 'park' it.

If you are homeless the council must look into your circumstances and if you are in priority need (see below) must give you help with housing.

I'm not homeless yet; do I qualify for help?

If you are likely to become homeless in the near future, apply to the council for accommodation as soon as possible. The Government has urged councils to take steps to help people such as yourself to avoid homelessness.

If you will become homeless within the next 28 days (e.g. because a possession order for your eviction will expire by then) the council must accept you as a person 'threatened' with homelessness and the help they must give depends on whether you are in priority need or became threatened with homelessness intentionally.

Am I in priority need?

There are four groups of priority need. Only the last of them specifically relates to disability.

You are in priority need if:

(a) you or someone you live with or might live with is pregnant *or*

(b) you have dependent children who live with or might live with you *or*

(c) you are homeless as a result of an emergency or disaster *or*

(d) you or someone you live with or might live with is *vulnerable* (this is the category you are most likely to be in if you are disabled)

If the council accept you as possibly being homeless and in priority need they must provide temporary accommodation for you while they are looking into your application for housing.

If they then decide you are homeless and in priority need they must provide you with some accommodation. For how long they have to house you depends on whether you became homeless intentionally (see below).

Do I qualify as 'vulnerable'?

You will be in priority need if you are 'vulnerable' or if someone you live with (or would normally live with) is vulnerable. The word is not defined in any Act of Parliament but a series of court cases has decided that you are vulnerable if you are *less well able to fend for yourself than an able-bodied person in getting or keeping accommodation or in dealing with homelessness.*

So it is not enough that you are disabled. That disability must in some way hamper you in dealing with housing. For example, if you are confined to bed or in hospital you will clearly experience problems in seeking accommodation whereas if you suffer from fits or seizures only at night you are unlikely to do so.

Nor is being 'vulnerable' enough just on its own. The reason for your vulnerability must be at least in part based on:

(a) physical disability *or*
(b) mental illness *or*
(c) mental handicap *or*
(d) old age *or*
(e) some other special reason.

It is the council housing staff who have to decide whether or not you are vulnerable and whether the reason is one of those listed.

They will usually refer your application for housing to a Medical Officer for advice. The Medical Officer will then approach your GP. You should make sure that your GP is aware that you are applying to the council for housing and is fully briefed about your disabilities. If you are seeing a specialist and feel his or her opinion might be helpful tell the council so that they can put their Medical Officer in touch with the specialist.

Once the council has a report on your disabilities (and their causes) from the Medical Officer they have to decide whether these make you 'vulnerable' in the way described above. If you have someone who is familiar with your disabilities and the problems you face in getting or keeping accommodation (e.g. a social worker or community nurse), tell the council so that they can be approached before the council makes a decision.

If the council decides that you are not vulnerable or otherwise in priority need, but that you are homeless, they must give you some help (advice and assistance) to find somewhere to stay. They might also consider you under the National Assistance Act (see below).

If the council decides you are vulnerable then the duty it owes to you depends on whether you are homeless intentionally.

Am I 'intentionally homeless'?
You can only be described as intentionally homeless if you had accommodation which met all three of the conditions mentioned on page 53 and you deliberately did something (or failed to do something) as a result of which you lost it. You would therefore be intentionally homeless if you deliberately destroyed or abandoned a perfectly good home (whether your own home or a council or private protected tenancy) or simply failed to pay the rent so that a court granted your landlord a possession order.

That action can only count against you if it was 'deliberate'. So if you were acting in ignorance or could not be responsible for your actions (e.g. you were acting unknowingly and under the influence of your disability) you cannot have become homeless intentionally.

The council will be trying to find out why it is you are homeless now. They are entitled to ignore any temporary accommodation you have had since your homelessness started (such as in hotels or temporary stays with friends) and will look instead at what happened to your last 'settled' home. It is only if you lost that in the way described above that you can be said to be intentionally homeless.

What if the council agrees I am homeless and not intentionally so and in priority need?

The law requires that they must provide you with accommodation indefinitely. Usually this will be by offering you a tenancy of a council house or flat, although you may have to be offered temporary accommodation until something suitable becomes available.

As an alternative the council could ask a housing association or the local social services department to provide you with the necessary accommodation. This is most likely if your disability affects the type of housing that is suitable for you and the council do not have such housing themselves. If neither the social services department nor a housing association can help, the council must take care of your housing needs themselves.

If the council find that you have no connection with their area (and nor does any member of your household) they can refer their housing obligation to a different council if you have (or a member of your household has) a connection with that other council. The council with which you do have a connection must then provide the housing.

What if the council agrees that I am homeless and in priority need but says that I am intentionally homeless?

In this case the law requires the council to provide accommodation for you for such a time as will give you a reasonable chance of finding accommodation yourself. You must also be given advice and assistance to help you in that search. The amount of time the council will give you in temporary accommodation will therefore depend on the ease with which you could reasonably find a home for yourself. This may only be a matter of weeks or months in some areas.

If the council has to provide me with housing (permanently or temporarily) what type of accommodation can I expect?

The law says that the accommodation offered to you must be 'suitable'. That means that it must be appropriate, having regard to what the council has found out about you while considering your application. So it must be a big enough unit to accommodate you, together with any people who are going to live with you, and it must be accessible to you having regard to your disability.

However, the council does not necessarily have to find accommodation which matches up to what you want in terms of location or nearby facilities. It will have done its legal duty if it simply offers you one unit of suitable accommodation even if it is not wholly to your liking.

How do I find out what decisions the council has reached?

Once consideration of your application has been concluded, the council must write to you with its decisions on the questions of whether you are homeless, have priority need or are intentionally homeless. If any of these are decided against you and the council is therefore not going to secure housing for you, you must be given the reasons. If you have no address to which the council can send this decision letter it must have a copy available for you to collect from the council's offices.

Can I challenge the decision the council has made?

There is no straightforward right of appeal to a court or tribunal against the decision the council makes on your application. If you feel the decision is wrong or unfair take your decision letter to one of the agencies mentioned in Chapter 11 for help and advice. They might suggest a review of your case by more senior council officers or councillors or they could arrange legal advice for you to challenge the council in court. You could also complain to the local Ombudsman (see page 131).

What is the 'National Assistance Act' procedure?

A law passed in 1948 requires a local authority to arrange accommodation for you if 'by reason of age, infirmity or any other circumstance' you are in need of care and attention not otherwise available to you. This might be because you have nowhere to live or because your present home is unsuitable. You are only entitled to claim this help with accommodation from the council in whose area you are normally resident (if you are not sure whether you fulfil the condition of normal residence, apply anyway and if turned down seek advice from one of the agencies listed in Chapter 11). You can apply under this procedure if you are disabled whatever age you are.

Because this procedure is for people who are in need of 'care and attention' the type of accommodation provided will usually be a residential care home which provides both care and accommodation for a number of people with the same needs that you have.

Your application will be considered by the council and an official will visit you to discuss the sort of accommodation you need and the range of care homes available. Your GP may also be able to offer useful advice. If the council accepts your application it will suggest a suitable home. You should then visit to satisfy yourself that it meets your needs and that you will get on with the other staff and residents.

If you take up the place offered, you will need to decide what to do about any accommodation you presently have. If you are a tenant you could give notice or see whether the tenancy can be passed on to other members of your family. Take advice from one of the agencies in Chapter 11 *before* deciding what to do about your former home. If you own your own home you can either sell it or keep it on with another member of your family or someone else living there. Before you make any permanent decision you should give the residential home a try to make sure you will be comfortable there.

The home will either be owned and run by the council or the council will have arranged a place for you in a home run by a voluntary organization or privately owned. Either way the council will assess a weekly charge that you pay to them. The government lays down the minimum amount and above that the local authority itself works out what you should pay. If you feel you are paying too much or have difficulty in meeting the charges, consult one of the agencies mentioned in Chapter 11.

If the council refuses to help you in the way that I have described there is no automatic right of appeal to a court or tribunal. The procedure for challenging the council's decision involves complaining to a Government minister. Any of the agencies described in Chapter 11 will be able to help you with this.

Are there any other ways I can get the council to help me with housing?

Yes, but they depend on your personal circumstances.

If you are losing your home because it is unfit and is being demolished or redeveloped you should ask the council for rehousing under the 'Land Compensation Act'.

If you have children and they are likely to go into care if you do not find a home for your family, ask at the Social Services Department of your local County or Regional Council for help with accommodation under the 'Child Care Act'.

If you are in need of housing as a result of some disaster such as a fire or flood, a local authority has power to provide accommodation for you (usually temporarily) under their emergency powers. Apply at the town hall.

If I choose to arrange residential care accommodation myself with a private or voluntary organization, can I get help with the cost?

It is up to you and the owners of the home you have chosen how much you will pay for staying there. Neither the Government nor the local council set maximum or minimum amounts for what can be charged. If you find that the charge is very high for a low level of care you should make inquiries of other homes in the area to see if there is somewhere else more suited to your needs and finances.

If you qualify for the benefit income support (see page 80), the social security office will include in your benefit an amount towards the fees charged by the home. There are limits to the amount they can pay so that there might be a shortfall between the amount you receive by way of benefit and the fees you have to pay. If this has happened to you, take the following steps. First, have your income support entitlement checked. Your local Citizens' Advice Bureau or one of the other agencies mentioned in Chapter 11 will gladly do this free of charge if you send them details of the fees at your home and the benefits you receive. Second, you could ask the Social Services

Department of your council if they will make 'topping-up' payments to meet the difference between the benefits you receive and the fees charged. Third, a charity or ex-service organization may be prepared to help meet the balance of the fees and this will not affect your income support at all – ask one of the agencies mentioned in Chapter 11 for details of appropriate organizations which might help in this way.

4. Benefits

What cash benefit do I qualify for if I am disabled?

In a perfect world the answer to this question would be simple – a disability benefit, which would provide regular and adequate financial support when needed. Regrettably, there is no such benefit. What you are entitled to from the social security system will probably be a mixture of various different benefits and allowances depending upon your personal circumstances and the extent of your disability.

If you are disabled or have a disabled person in your household you or they are probably entitled to one or more of the benefits which I have divided into the following groups (each of the benefits is more fully described later in this chapter):

Group A (pages 65–72): straightforward disability benefits paid without a means test or national insurance contributions. This group includes attendance allowance, mobility allowance, invalid care allowance and severe disablement allowance. The most important condition for claiming is usually the extent and effect of your disability.

Group B (pages 73–8): benefits provided under the National Insurance (NI) Scheme for which entitlement depends on your record of NI contributions. These benefits include sickness benefit, invalidity benefit and unemployment benefit. They are normally paid irrespective of your savings or other income and additional amounts are paid with some of them if you have dependents.

Group C (pages 78–90): means-tested benefits. These are designed to ensure that everyone in the community can have a basic minimum income. They include income support (for those not working full time), family credit (for people in full-time work) and housing benefit (for help with housing costs). How much you are entitled to receive depends on your family size and circumstances, your income and savings.

Group D (pages 90–93): benefits from specific schemes. Special benefits are paid without contributions or means-tests to specific groups of people under special schemes. These include the War Pension Scheme (see pages 9–10) and the Industrial Industries Scheme (page 26).

Group E (pages 93–5) benefits paid by employers. Some cash benefits are now paid directly by employers who then reclaim the money from the Government. You receive these benefits without regard to your income or contribution records. They include statutory sick pay and statutory maternity pay.

How can I make sure I claim the right benefits for my family and myself?

Look over the rest of this chapter to get a general idea of what the different benefits are and which of them might be of relevance to you. Then pick up DSS leaflet FB 28 *Sick or Disabled* (from your local main post office or social security office or telephone Freeline DSS on 0800 666 555). It describes the benefits you might be entitled to and contains an order form for detailed leaflets on each specific benefit.

When you have read this it might seem that you are entitled to several different benefits from each of the Groups set out above. However, although many benefits can be combined, several of them overlap so that claiming one can reduce or wipe out another.

After scanning this chapter, you might find it helpful to get some free advice about the best things to claim. You could start by telephoning the DSS Freeline on 0800 666 555 (for Northern Ireland the number is 0800 616 757).

They will give you general advice and the address of your local social security office at which to make your claims.

If you would prefer some independent advice, a face-to-face talk with someone who knows about benefits, or simply help with filling in the claim forms, contact your local Citizens' Advice Bureau or one of the other advice agencies listed in Chapter 11. Again that help is free of charge.

Even if you are already receiving one or more of the benefits described in this book it is worth having the help of someone else to check that you are receiving all you are entitled to. Many thousands of disabled people miss out on benefits because they do not claim the right ones. Don't forget that it costs nothing to make a claim, so if in any doubt about whether you might be entitled put in a claim.

If you are in urgent need of cash help apply for income support (which is described below) at your local DSS office. You can get the address from your local library, main post office or the telephone book. You will need the claim form A1 which will be sent to you by the social security office on request. (If you are registering as unemployed ask for the equivalent form, B1, at the Unemployment Benefit Office.) This will ensure that you have at least some income while you are considering – or claiming for – other benefits.

GROUP A BENEFITS

What are the Group A Benefits?
These are benefits intended to provide cash help to those with disabilities. You can claim them whether or not you have paid National Insurance contributions and regardless of what other income and savings you have. The main conditions you have to satisfy will be to do with your disability and its effect. The three main benefits are

attendance allowance, invalid care allowance and mobility allowance. It is quite possible for your family to receive all three of these allowances. There is also a separate severe disablement allowance. An outline of each benefit is given below together with a reference to the leaflet which gives more details. If you want fuller information on all the Group A benefits there is a Government handbook *Non-contributory Benefits for Disabled People* (DSS) available from HMSO and main bookshops.

Can I claim attendance allowance?

Yes, if you are severely disabled (physically or mentally) and your disability means that you need the help of someone else to care for you. You don't have to have someone caring for you at the moment. It is the fact that you *need* care that is important. You must have needed such help for 6 months before you qualify.

If your claim succeeds you receive a tax-free weekly allowance at one of two rates (each worth over £1000 a year) depending on how much care you need. You can use the money in any way you want although many disabled people use it to help pay for the services of a carer. You can never be too old to make a claim but the allowance cannot be paid for a child under the age of two.

If you think you *might* be entitled, make a claim as soon as possible because the allowance cannot usually be backdated. You can get the claim form and combined explanatory leaflet (NI 205) from the local social security office. If you can't easily get to the office (or have someone pick up the leaflet for you) don't worry – just write to your nearest DSS office and say that you want to claim attendance allowance. They will then send you the form and when you return it they will treat your claim as made from the date they got your first letter.

To get the allowance, the formal requirements you must satisfy are that *either* during the day or during the night you need regular help with bodily functions such as dressing, eating, washing, using the toilet, etc. *or* you need someone to be on the look-out to see you do not harm yourself or others (for example, to help you if you have fits or falls).

When they get your claim, the DSS will arrange for a doctor to come and see you at home to prepare a report on your condition. You can prepare for the doctor's visit by making a list of all the things you need help with. You could also let the DSS have a note of all the times you have needed help in the week or two before the visit (but keep a copy).

When they receive the doctor's report, the DSS decides your claim and if you satisfy the conditions you will be sent a payment book for the allowance, which you can cash at the post office or, if you prefer, the money can be paid straight into a bank account.

If your claim is refused (or you get the lower rather than the higher rate) don't be too disheartened. There is a simple procedure for having a second look at your claim – it's called a *review*. Many people who are turned down the first time are eventually awarded the benefit if they ask for a review. The decision letter you receive explains how to go about asking for a review. The Disability Alliance (address in Chapter 11) have a useful leaflet called *Attendance Allowance – Going for a Review*.

Once you have the allowance, it will go on being paid indefinitely for as long as you satisfy the conditions (but it will not be paid during long stays in hospital).

Attendance allowance will not be enough to live on by itself. You could supplement it with earnings and, if you qualify for it, you will probably also be entitled to some of the other benefits described below. In fact there are some benefits for which the allowance positively helps you to qualify and there are no benefits which are reduced because you get attendance allowance.

Because you can only qualify for this benefit if you need the help of someone else you might find it useful to read Chapter 9 on Carers and Caring.

What is invalid care allowance?

This is paid to people who look after a disabled person claiming attendance allowance. The idea is that it makes up for the fact that, because of spending their time caring for a disabled person, they cannot take a full-time job. Invalid care allowance (ICA) is a weekly cash allowance (worth over £1000 a year) and people claiming it are credited with National Insurance contributions as well. Extra is paid if the carer has adult or child dependants.

You qualify for ICA if you spend at least 35 hours a week looking after a person who gets attendance allowance (as described above) or an attendance allowance under similar schemes for war disablement (pages 9–10) or industrial disablement (page 26). You don't have to be living with the disabled person or related to them but many people getting ICA are in fact looking after their disabled spouses or disabled children.

You can get the claim form, combined explanatory leaftet (NI 212) and a pre-paid envelope addressed to the ICA Claims Unit from the local DSS office (by either visiting, writing to or telephoning the office).

If you have satisfied the conditions for some time but not previously made a claim you can ask for the allowance to be backdated for up to a year. If the allowance is refused you have a right of appeal to an independent tribunal and one of the agencies mentioned in Chapter 11 might be able to help you with the appeal.

You cannot qualify if you are a full-time student or if you are working full time. Part-time work which brings in a modest amount each week is ignored. To claim you must be between 16 and 65 if you are a man, 16 and 60 if you are a woman. If you are a woman aged 60–65, take advice from one of the agencies mentioned in Chapter 11 about making a claim. The allowance will not be paid if you are receiving certain other benefits (such as widow's benefits or retirement pension) and, even if awarded, it will not on its own provide enough to live on. You will usually be able to top it up by claiming one or more of the Group C benefits (see below) or by earnings from a small amount of part-time work.

Can I claim mobility allowance?

Yes, if your disability means that you find it very difficult to walk or you cannot walk at all. The allowance is a tax-free weekly cash benefit (worth over £1000 per year) designed to help you pay for the extra costs of transport you will have as a result of your disability (although you are free to spend it as you choose).

There are three alternative ways to qualify, either:

(a) you cannot walk at all *or*

(b) your ability to walk is so restricted that you are 'virtually unable to walk' *or*

(c) you are able to walk but if you did so the exertion would seriously damage your health.

You must show that these conditions will apply for a year or more and that they stem from a physical disability (including a physical condition causing mental handicap) rather than from mental disabilities alone.

To claim this allowance you must not have reached your 66th birthday. A child cannot qualify until its fifth birthday (although a claim can be put in in advance). You must be a UK resident and have been in the UK for at least a year in the last 18 months. You must be able to make use of the allowance if it is awarded to you (for example, you cannot qualify if you cannot leave your home).

You can get the claim form and the explanatory leaflet (NI 211) from your local social security office. The allowance cannot be backdated so you should claim as soon as possible if you think you *might* be entitled. Once the office receives and has acknowledged your claim, the Mobility Allowance Unit will arrange for you to be seen by a local doctor (not usually your own GP). The examination will either be at the doctor's surgery or at your own home. The doctor then reports back to the Unit on your walking ability. You can prepare for the examination by making a list of all the difficulties you have with walking (or trying to walk) to give to the doctor (keep a copy). You could also ask someone you know to do a walking test with you to see how you get on. Your companion should make a note of how far you walked (and the difficulties you experienced) so that this can be given to the doctor too.

The benefit will be awarded for a fixed period (minimum one year). The longest period that can be awarded is one ending with your 80th birthday.

If you are refused the allowance you have a right of appeal to an independent tribunal. If the appeal is about the medical conditions (i.e. your walking ability) it is heard by a Medical Appeal Tribunal. Appeals about other aspects (e.g. the residence conditions) are heard by the Social Security Appeals Tribunal. The agencies mentioned in Chapter 11 will be able to help you with any appeal.

Mobility allowance on its own will not provide an income enough to live on but it is very useful to have as it can be paid even if you are receiving other benefits or even earnings. Getting the allowance can never lead to a reduction in your entitlement to other benefits and allowances.

What is severe disablement allowance?

Despite its name, this is not a benefit automatically paid to all severely disabled people. It is a weekly tax-free cash benefit (worth over £1000 a year) payable if you are severely disabled (mentally or physically) *and* have been continuously incapable of work for 28 weeks *and* have not paid enough National Insurance contributions to qualify for invalidity benefit (which is more generous and is discussed in Group B).

You are likely to want to claim the allowance if you have not had a recent record of paying National Insurance contributions in employment or self-employment – possibly because you were disabled at a young age or you are a disabled woman whose main work has been raising a family. But if you are incapable of work as a result of an injury at work or a work-related disease, claim sickness benefit instead (see Group B) and then industrial disablement benefits (see Group D, described on page 90).

To claim you must be aged between 16 and 60 if you are a woman, 16 and 65 if you are a man. If you are a woman between the ages of 60 and 65 take advice from one of the agencies in Chapter 11. You must be in Britain and have past residence in Britain. You must have been incapable of work for 28 weeks before the allowance can be paid.

If you think you fulfil these conditions you *also* have to show that you are severely disabled. You can do this in any one of the following ways:

(a) you have been incapable of work since before you reached your 20th birthday *or*

(b) you are receiving a mobility or attendance allowance (explained above) *or*

(c) you are registered blind or partially sighted (see pages 119–123) *or*

(d) you have received a vaccine damage payment (see page 9) *or*

(e) you have an invalid car, tricycle, or car allowance from DSS (see pages 108–9) *or*

(f) you are accepted to be 80% disabled.

If the only condition you might fulfil is the last one, see pages 27–8 for an explanation of how percentages of disablement are worked out. If you are assessed at 75% disabled this is rounded-up to 80% so that you qualify.

As you can see, there are a lot of conditions. If you think you *might* be able to meet some of them – put in a claim. You don't have to be absolutely sure. You can get the combined claim form and explanatory leaflet (NI 252) from your local social security office. If you can only qualify on the grounds that you are 80% disabled the DSS will arrange for your claim to be referred to an independent doctor (or perhaps two doctors together) for an assessment of your disabilities.

If you qualify for the benefit you will be awarded a weekly amount for yourself and (depending on your partners' earnings, if any) extra for any dependent adults or children. Severe disability allowance can be paid on top of any salary or sick pay you are getting from your employer and any 'therapeutic earnings' (see page 76) you receive. If you get SDA there will be some benefits you cannot receive and for other benefits it will be taken into account before deciding how much you should be paid.

If you are refused SDA you have a right of appeal to an independent Social Security Appeal Tribunal (or, if the dispute is about the percentage of your disability, a Medical Appeal Tribunal). Any of the agencies mentioned in Chapter 11 could help you with an appeal.

On its own SDA will not provide you with enough to live on. If you have a low household income you may need to top it up with other benefits, especially one or more of those described in Group C.

GROUP B BENEFITS

What are the Group B benefits?

These are benefits you can qualify for if you have a record of paying National Insurance contributions (or of having received NI credited contributions). They are available to rich and poor alike and are designed to meet the need for extra financial help if certain circumstances arise. The main benefits are paid in respect of unemployment, long or short term sickness, retirement or widowhood.

Each of the benefits has specific conditions and they are described in outline below. Each of my descriptions includes references to the information leaflet from which you can get more details. Unfortunately, many of the benefit rules are complicated. If you want the fullest information you could look in your local library for the *Rights Guide to Non-Meanstested Benefits* published by the Child Poverty Action Group or the *Disability Rights Handbook* from the Disability Alliance. Both books are completely re-written every year so make sure you look at the current edition.

The primary condition for all of the following benefits is that you have paid enough National Insurance contributions of the right type at the right time. Don't worry about checking on that first – if you think the descriptions below apply to you just put in your claim and let the DSS work out if your record is sufficient.

Can I claim unemployment benefit?

You can claim unemployment benefit for each day on which you do not work but are capable of and available for work. The maximum you can claim for is 6 days in each week and the maximum number of days you can be paid for altogether in one spell of unemployment is 312 (which is 52 weeks of 6 days).

Unemployment benefit is paid fortnightly by giro-cheque sent to your home address. The basic benefit is worth £1500 a year and you can claim more if you have a dependent adult (depending on your partner's earnings if any) or dependent children (depending on *your* age).

You make your claim by going to the local Unemployment Benefit Office (you can get the address from the phone book, your local post office or library). You will be given forms to fill in and you may be interviewed about your claim and the circumstances which have led to your being unemployed. You will be asked to come back to the office regularly (probably every fortnight) to renew your claim for benefit – this is called 'signing on'.

Although you cannot usually be paid for the first three days of unemployment you should go to the office and make a claim as soon as you become unemployed.

Notice that you must be *capable* of work. If the DSS feel that your disability means that you are not really fit to take a job they will refuse your claim for unemployment benefit and suggest that you claim one of the benefits paid to people who are incapable of work. This is quite likely to happen if you had a job but lost it through sickness or took ill health retirement. You can challenge this decision (see below).

You must also be *available* to take work on the days for which you claim benefit. This means that if you are capable of work but have a disabled dependant or dependent children you will have to make definite arrangements for them to be cared for if you are offered work so that you can start work on 24 hours notice.

If you lost your job because of misconduct or you left voluntarily, without a good reason, your benefit can be withheld for up to six months as a penalty. If this happens to you or you are refused benefit altogether you have a right of appeal to an independent tribunal. The agencies mentioned in Chapter 11 may be able to help with an appeal.

Should you still be claiming benefit after six months you will be asked to attend an interview to discuss training and employment opportunities (called a Restart interview). If suitable employment or training opportunities are found for you but you fail to take them up, your benefit could be suspended.

On its own, unemployment benefit will not provide you with enough to live on. If you have a low household income you may need to top it up with other benefits, especially one or more of those described in Group C.

Should I be claiming sickness benefit?

You can claim sickness benefit if you are *incapable of work*. If you had a job when you became sick you should receive statutory sick pay from your employer (see page 94). This is worth more than sickness benefit and covers the same period so that you should try and get statutory sick pay from your employer first. If for some reason your employer thinks you are not eligible for statutory sick pay (if, for example you have already used up your entitlement) they will give you a form with which you can make your claim for sickness benefit.

If you were not working when you became ill (or you were self-employed) or your employer has given you a certificate that you are not entitled to statutory sick pay, you should claim sickness benefit as soon as you are incapable of work (whether or not you would be going to work if you were fit).

Remember that this is a Group B benefit so whether you get it or not will depend on your record of National Insurance contributions (unless your illness is caused by an accident at work or a work-related disease).

You will start getting sickness benefit as soon as you have been incapable of work for four days in a row. The benefit is paid on a weekly basis and is worth more than £1500 a year tax-free. If you have adult or child dependants you may be paid extra amounts for them (depending on your partner's earnings (if any) and your age) and for as long as you are claiming you will be credited with National Insurance contributions. All the details are in DSS leaflet NI 16 *Sickness Benefit* available from your social security office.

You make your claim by sending in evidence of your incapacity for work to your local social security office. In the first place you do this by completing form SC 1 which you can get at your doctor's surgery, hospital or DSS office. Later the evidence you send in will be the medical certificates which your GP (or hospital doctor) gives you.

As long as you are sending in certificates you will go on receiving sickness benefit for the whole time you are incapable of work. If you are still incapable of work after 28 weeks you will transfer on to invalidity benefit (see below).

If you feel that you might be able to manage some work under medical supervision or that a little work might positively help your recovery, the rules allow you to do a job and still claim sickness benefit. There are two conditions for this: first, you must tell the social security office in advance and second, your earnings each week must not come to more than a set amount (called the *therapeutic earnings* limit).

On its own, sickness benefit will not provide you with enough to live on. If you have a low household income you may need to top it up with other benefits, especially one or more of those described in Group C.

Could I claim invalidity benefit?

Yes, if you have been incapable of working for 28 weeks. Invalidity benefit is designed for people who have been incapable of work for more than 6 months and during that time have received statutory sick pay or sickness benefit. If you are a widow or widower and have been incapable of work that long you may be able to claim invalidity benefit without having claimed statutory sick pay or sickness benefit first.

Invalidity benefit is paid on a weekly basis by an order book which you cash at the post office. The basic benefit is tax-free and worth more than £2000 a year. There are extra amounts if you became ill before you were 55 (for a woman) or 60 (for a man) and if you have adults or children who are dependent on you. If you are a man and became ill between the ages of 55 and 60, take advice from one of the agencies mentioned in Chapter 11. The full details are in free leaflet N 116A *Invalidity Benefit*, available from your social security office.

The procedure for claiming is very easy. If you are receiving statutory sick pay your employer will give you a claim form several weeks before SSP runs out. If you are getting sickness benefit the DSS just transfers you on to invalidity benefit. After that you can carry on getting invalidity benefit for as long as you send in medical certificates right up until pension age (and then even longer if you defer your retirement).

You can carry on claiming even while you do some 'therapeutic work' but the conditions for that are the same as for sickness benefit (see above).

All the time you claim you must be 'incapable of work'. On each of your medical certificates your GP confirms whether you are or not. Sometimes the DSS will want to check whether the doctor's view is right and you could be called in for an examination by the Department's own doctors. Most often they will simply confirm your own doctor's view. However, if your invalidity benefit is stopped because of an unfavourable medical opinion ask your own doctor to keep giving you medical certificates and get advice from one of the agencies listed in Chapter 11.

Can I claim widow's benefits or retirement pension?

Disabled people get no special help in qualifying for widow's benefits (paid only to women) or retirement pension. The same rules apply as for able-bodied people.

If you are approaching pension age (60 for a woman, 65 for a man) send off to Age Concern (address in Chapter 11) for their booklet *Your Rights* which contains all the information you will need.

If someone in your family has died you can get good advice about the benefits position from DSS leaflet D 49 *What to Do After a Death*. You can get a copy at the office where you register the death, or from your local social security office. There is a leaflet FB 29 *Help When Someone Dies*, available from main post offices.

On its own neither a widow's nor a retirement pension will provide enough to live on as a disabled person. If you have a low household income you may need to top it up with other benefits, especially one or more of those described in Group C.

GROUP C BENEFITS

What are the Group C Benefits?

These are cash benefits paid to make sure everyone has a minimum level of regular income. The three main ones are family credit (which is for families in work), income support (for anyone not working full time) and housing benefit (for people with responsibility for housing costs). Most people drawing family credit or income support also receive housing benefit.

These benefits are paid because there is a legal entitlement to them. All three are means-tested which involves the authorities considering your family circumstances, income and savings. As a disabled person (or with a disabled person in your household) you are likely to be eligible to claim at least one of them.

Should I claim family credit?
Yes, if you are raising a family on a low wage because this is the benefit designed for working families with modest incomes.

If you are working at less than three-quarters of your normal earning capacity as a result of a disability you could also claim income support (see below). If this applies to you, take some advice from one of the agencies mentioned in Chapter 11 as to which would be the best of the two benefits for you to claim.

To qualify for family credit you must satisfy the following straightforward conditions

(a) you (or your partner) normally work 24 hours or more a week *and*

(b) you are bringing up a child or young person *and*

(c) you (and your partner) have less than £6000 savings *and*

(d) you are in Great Britain.

If you can satisfy all four conditions you can claim family credit, whether you are working for yourself or for an employer. How much you get (and whether you get anything at all) depends on your family income each week and the ages of your children.

What you receive is a payment book to be cashed each week at the post office. If contains payments for 26 weeks all for the same amount as calculated when you claimed. Before the book expires you can renew the claim and have your next 26 weeks based on circumstances at the date of the renewal, and repeat this every six months onwards.

You claim on form FC 1 (FCS 1 in Northern Ireland) which you can get from main post offices or your local social security office. It costs nothing to make a claim so you should have a go even if you only think you *might* be entitled. You should also get leaflet FB 27 *Bringing Up Children* which outlines family credit and all the other help available to families with children.

If you want chapter and verse about family credit ask your local DSS office for leaflet NI 261 *A Guide to Family Credit* – it has all the details.

Should I claim income support?

Hundreds of thousands of disabled people and their dependants claim income support every week. For a lot of them this benefit is the main source of income (it used to be called supplementary benefit) – for others it just tops up other monies they have coming in.

Normally to be eligible for income support you have to meet each of the following conditions. But they are each modified to make the benefit easier for disabled people to claim as I explain below:

1. you are not working 24 hours or more a week
2. your partner, if you have one, is not working 24 hours or more a week
3. your savings (including those of any partner) are less than £6000
4. you are available for work
5. you are in Great Britain
6. you are not a full-time student
7. you are 18 or older.

If you fulfil each of these conditions (perhaps with the help of the modifications for disabled people and their carers described below) you should certainly claim income support. You can start the process by filling in the slip in the leaflet SB 1 *Income Support – Cash Help* which you can get from your local post office. They will give you the address of the correct social security office to send it to. The DSS will then send you the application form. It's a bit long but don't let it put you off. You have a legal right to the money and it costs nothing to make a claim. If you think you might be entitled you should apply. (If you or your partner are signing on for work at an Unemployment Benefit Office ask for the application form B.)

If you suddenly realize as a result of looking at this list that you have fulfilled these conditions for some time don't panic. Just put in your claim as soon as possible and explain why you didn't claim earlier. You could get arrears for up to one year.

If your claim is successful you will be sent regular giro-cheque payments of benefit or an order book you cash at the post office of your choice.

What are the modifications which help disabled people and their carers to qualify for income support?

Each of the seven conditions for qualifying (set out above) is modified for some disabled people and their carers.

Conditions 1 & 2. The normal rule is that neither you nor your partner can work 24 hours or more a week. But if you are mentally or physically disabled, and, as a result, your earning capacity is less than three-quarters of what it would otherwise have been, it doesn't matter how many hours you work. For example, you put in a 27 hour week and earn £50 but had you not been disabled you could have worked a 35 hour week and earned £75 – you can still claim income support.

For carers, the modification is that if you claim invalid care allowance (see above) or look after a person who has applied for or been awarded attendance allowance it doesn't matter how many hours of paid work you do, you can still claim income support.

Condition 3. The normal rule is that you can't claim income support if you and your partner have combined savings or other 'capital' of over £6000. There are lots of rules about the types of capital which do and don't count in adding up to £6000. Two are specially relevant if you are disabled:

(a) any money made up of arrears of attendance or mobility allowance is ignored for one year from the date you were paid the arrears.

(b) if any money you have is a trust fund set up to compensate for an injury (for example one of the forms of compensation described in Chapter 1) its value will be ignored for at least 2 years after you claim and if the fund is for a child of yours it will be ignored indefinitely.

Condition 4. The normal rule is that to claim income support you must be available for work. There are lots of exceptions to the rule and several are especially relevant to disabled people. You do not have to be available for work if:

(a) you are incapable of work as a result of some disease or physical or mental disability *or*

(b) as a result of physical or mental disablement your earning capacity is less than three-quarters of what it would have been *or*

(c) you are a student and your job prospects are reduced on account of mental or physical disability *or*

(d) you are registered blind (see pages 119–123) or have regained eyesight within the last 28 weeks *or*

(e) you are a carer, and the person you are caring for has claimed (or is receiving) attendance allowance *or*

(f) you receive invalid care allowance.

If you meet any of these qualifying conditions you can get income support without being available for work.

Condition 5. The normal rule is that you cannot receive income support unless you are in Great Britain. There are some exceptions which allow people temporarily leaving Britain to carry on getting benefit for up to 4 weeks. For example, if you are incapable of work and you go abroad for treatment for that incapacity you will get income support for the first 4 weeks you are away.

Condition 6. The normal rule is that students cannot claim income support. If you are 18 and still in school-type education you cannot usually claim income support (your parents claim child benefit for you instead). But there are several exceptions. Among them are two related to disability. First, you can claim income support if your disability means that you would be unlikely to find a job within 12 months if you were looking for one rather than studying. Second, you can claim if you are effectively maintaining yourself because your parent or parents live away from you and are themselves chronically sick or disabled.

If you are 19 or over and studying full time you are not usually entitled to claim income support other than during the summer holidays but as a disabled student you can carry on claiming income support all year round if your disability means it would take you an unreasonable length of time to find a job compared to how long it would take able-bodied students.

Condition 7 Normally a person must be 18 or over to claim income support but there are exceptions, including some relevant to disabled young people. A 16 or 17-year-old can claim income support if he or she has left school-type education and is:

(a) blind *or*

(b) incapable of work or training *or*

(c) are caring for a disabled person

If they are still in school-type education they can claim if they are:

(a) disabled such that they would be unlikely to find a job within 12 months if looking for one rather than studying *or*

(b) effectively maintaining themselves because their parents are not living with them as a result of parents' own chronic sickness or disability.

How much income support will I get?

As a disabled person (or with a disabled person in your household) you should qualify for more benefit than an able-bodied person in the same circumstances. The DSS work out how much you are going to get by going through the following stages:

(a) they look at the amount the Government has set down for your family (called *personal allowances*) *then*

(b) they add to that any special amounts (called *premiums*) you might be entitled to, *then*

(c) they add any amount you qualify for towards your *housing costs, then*

(d) from the total of those three things they deduct other money you have coming in each week, *then*

(e) the balance is paid to you as income support.

This sounds very simple but there are lots of detailed rules about how the calculation should be done. Even with the best will in the world the DSS will make mistakes from time to time – either simple maths errors or by leaving out various sums you are entitled to. Therefore you should always check the amount of income support you are awarded is in fact correct. It is quite simple to do this. Just write a short note to your local DSS office and ask them to send you form A124 – this gives a detailed breakdown of how your benefit was worked out. You could then check this through yourself or ask one of the agencies mentioned in Chapter 11 for help in doing so.

You need to look over all the steps in the calculation. Watch out for the following:

Personal Allowances
These vary according to your age and whether you are single, a lone parent or have a partner. If you have children there are different amounts according to their ages. Make sure all your family members are included in the list with the right ages.

Premiums

These vary according to your circumstances. As a disabled person or with a disabled person in your household look out for the following:

(a) if you have a disabled child or young person living with you you should receive the family premium (because you have children) plus a *disabled child premium* for each disabled child. If you are a lone parent you will also get the lone parent premium. Your child qualifies for the disabled child premium if he or she:

(i)   gets attendance allowance *or*

(ii) gets mobility allowance *or*

(iii) would be getting one of those benefits but is in hospital *or*

(iv) is registered blind *or*

(v)   was registered blind and has regained sight within the last 28 weeks *and*

(vi) has less than £3000 savings of his or her own (money in trust to compensate for disablement does not count).

If your child is disabled there is much more help available than just income support (see Chapter 6).

(b) if you are disabled yourself, you qualify for an extra premium if you fall into any of the following categories (this is in addition to any family premium or lone parent premium you might qualify for if you have children):

(i) you are registered blind or were registered blind but have regained your sight within the last 28 weeks *or*

(ii) you get any of the following benefits: attendance allowance (page 66), constant attendance allowance (page 29), mobility allowance (page 69), mobility supplement (page 107), invalidity benefit (page 76), severe disablement allowance (page 70) *or* help under the old invalid vehicle scheme (page 107), *or*

(iii) you have been incapable of work for 28 weeks and

you are still incapable of work.

If you fulfil any of these conditions the extra premium you are entitled to is the *disabled persons premium* (if you are under 60) or the *higher pensioner premium* (if you are over 60). The premiums are higher if you have a partner whether your partner is disabled or not.

(c) if you are disabled yourself and need a carer you might qualify for a *severe disability premium* in addition to the ordinary one for disabled people. To qualify you must:

(i)   be getting attendance allowance (or constant attendance allowance) *and*

(ii) not have a carer who receives invalid care allowance looking after you *and*

(iii) be living 'alone'

If you think you meet these conditions you should certainly ask for this extra premium to be included in your benefit. (You might also be eligible for help from the Independent Living Fund (see page 126)).

(d) if it is your partner who is disabled (rather than you) it may be more advantageous to you if he or she is the person claiming income support rather than you. This is because you cannot claim on the basis of your partner's disability the ordinary disability premium (on the 'incapable of work ground') or the severe disability premium. You can get advice about whether to 'swop' claimants from one of the agencies mentioned in Chapter 11.

(e) if both you and your partner are disabled you can only get one lot of the ordinary disability premiums (which are higher anyway if you are a couple) but if you both qualify you can get two sets of severe disability premium (although the conditions are modified slightly for couples).

Housing Costs

Your income support will not include amounts for your

rent, rates or community charge. You get help with these through rebate schemes (see housing benefit (page 88)). Your income support will cover other housing costs such as some mortgage and home-loan repayments. Normally this amount will be reduced to take account of any non-dependants in your home (such as grown up children). But if you are disabled no deduction should be made in respect of these other people if you or your partner are:

(a) getting any type of attendance allowance *or*

(b) registered blind (or within 28 weeks of having recovered eyesight).

Your Income

The rules about what income counts and therefore is deducted from your income support entitlement are long and complicated. Here I mention some which are particularly important if you (or someone in your family) is disabled. In those circumstances, the following sources of income do not count and should *not* be deducted from your entitlement:

(a) mobility allowance or mobility supplement

(b) any attendance allowances

(c) any ex-gratia payments awarded instead of these benefits

(d) the first £5 of any war disablement pension (page 10)

(e) any payment you receive from a council, health authority or organization for offering temporary (respite) care

(f) any payment from the Macfarlane Trust (page 11) or Independent Living Fund (p. 126).

Once you have checked over your income support assessment to see that these points have been covered, if you are dissatisfied you can ask the DSS to look again at their assessment (this is called a review) or you can appeal to an independent tribunal.

Where can I find out more about income support?

I have made some suggestions on pages 64-5 about getting social security advice generally. If you want a free detailed summary of the whole income support scheme ask at a DSS office for free leaflet SB 20 *A Guide to Income Support.*

If you dispute any decision made by the DSS about your income support and need advice contact one of the agencies mentioned in Chapter 11.

Should I claim housing benefit?

If you pay rent, rates or the community charge you should certainly consider claiming housing benefit.

Just like income support, entitlement to housing benefit is worked out according to your family size, your savings, your income and amounts of benefit which the Government lays down. But, unlike income support, your right to housing benefit is worked out by your local council not by the social security office.

If you qualify for income support and you claim housing benefit the help you will receive can cover as much as the whole of your rent and up to 80% of any community charge or general rates that you have to pay (see below). A claim form is included with the forms for income support and when you apply the social security office will send the housing benefit form on to the council for you.

If you are not claiming or receiving income support, you should get the housing benefit claim form from your council's housing department or the town hall.

What type of housing benefit you receive and how it is paid depends on whether you are an owner-occupier (page 32), a council tenant (page 46), or a tenant renting from a private landlord (page 40), or housing association (page 45). A brief outline of how housing benefit applies is given in each of the sections referred to above, and you can get appropriate details for your situation from either the *Owner-Occupiers Handbook, The Private Tenants Handbook* or *The Public Tenants Handbook,* all of which are published in this series.

How much housing benefit will I get?

This depends on your personal circumstances and in particular the amount of community charge, rent or rates you pay.

Rather than try to calculate your own entitlement, the best thing to do is put in a claim and see what happens. Although it may be a few weeks before you hear from the council, they will work out whether you are entitled and let you have a written decision. It costs nothing to claim and millions of pounds of benefit are lost every year just because people (many of them disabled) fail to have a go and claim.

If you are awarded enough money to meet any rent *in full* and 80% of your community charge or rates you will not need to check the council's calculation because in normal cases this is the most they can award. However, if you are left to pay 20% of your rates and would like help towards that amount you can ask the council to award you more than the normal housing benefit. They can do this if they are persuaded that your circumstances are 'exceptional'. To get this extra help write to the housing benefit office and outline why your circumstances are exceptional – for example, mention that you are disabled and specify any extra costs and difficulties involved. If you are refused extra help towards the 20% of rates, ask one of the agencies mentioned in Chapter 11 to help you with an appeal.

If you get *less* housing benefit than the amount needed to cover your rent in full and/or 80% of the community charge, write to the council and ask for a breakdown of how your benefit has been calculated so you can check it through. When you get the breakdown you will need to check whether the council has included the special modifications allowed to the normal rules for disabled people, in particular:

(a) does the calculation include any disability premium or severe disability premium that you may be entitled to (see pages 85–6 for what this means)?

(b) has any disabled persons rate relief been allowed for (see pages 37–9)?

(c) have any non-dependent adults been taken into account when perhaps they should have been left out of account. (e.g. because you are blind or they are caring for you)?

The best thing to do is take the calculation sheet to one of the advice centres mentioned in Chapter 11 to have it checked. If they find that all the calculations are correct and the necessary modifications have been taken into account they can nevertheless help you put in a claim for extra help based on your exceptional circumstances. This procedure is explained above.

GROUP D BENEFITS

What are the Group D Benefits?

These are benefits paid by the social security system (or with money from that system) to meet particular needs. Most have no means test or rules about National Insurance contributions. However, one of the problems with social security is that there are so many different schemes. What I provide below is a short summary of each of the different schemes together with a reference to where you can get more details. Run down the list and see if any of the headings apply to your situation and put in an application if you think you might be entitled:

Disabled in Military Service or Wartime.
There is a special scheme of war disablement benefits.
This is described on pages 9–11 of this book.

Disabled at Work or Suffering from an Industrial Disease
There is a special scheme of industrial disablement benefits described on pages 26–9 of this book.

Disabled Children
There is a fund providing financial help to adults raising
children with severe disabilities. This is called the Family
Fund and the details are on pages 12, 104). (See also
Chapter 6 generally for more information on youngsters
with disabilities.)

Disabled as a Result of NHS Vaccination
There is a special scheme of compensation called the
Vaccine Damage payments scheme. Details are on page 9.

Raising Children
Child benefit is available to everyone raising children.
The details are on page 103. If you are raising children
alone you could claim one parent benefit as well. You can
get details and a claim form for that benefit in leaflet
CH11 available free from your local main post office or
social security office.

Christmas Bonus
A small lump sum payment is made in the weeks before
Christmas to recipients of various social security benefits.
A double payment is made to some married couples. The
bonus is usually paid automatically without the need for a
separate claim and is tax-free.

Funeral Payments
A person receiving income support, housing benefit or

family credit is eligible for a grant towards any funeral expenses they have to bear. The grant is not repayable but the social security office will be reimbursed from the estate (if any) left by the deceased person. To claim, ask at your social security office for claim form SF 200.

Maternity Payments

If you have just adopted or had a new baby in your family you can claim a lump sum grant if you are receiving income support or family credit. To claim ask at your local social security office for claim form SF 100.

Cold Weather Payments

If you receive income support and your benefit includes the pensioner or disability premiums (see page 86) or you have a child under two, you are entitled to extra cash to help in periods of exceptionally cold weather. To claim, contact your local social security office. Announcements will be made in your local newspaper if the Government accept that the weather has been cold enough for payments to be made.

AIDS

There is no special social security benefit for people with AIDS but people who are haemophiliac and received transfusions of infected blood can claim help with financial expenses from a special trust fund (see page 11).

Travel Costs

There are a range of schemes for financial help with travel costs and they are outlined in Chapter 7.

Lump Sum Payments

As a disabled person you will from time to time face one-off expenses such as the need to replace clothing, furniture and other household items. If you receive income support you will probably not have enough regular income to save towards such eventualities. Therefore a scheme called the Social Fund is available to you at the local social security office. You can claim grants from the scheme. These don't have to be paid back and will be paid to meet the need for something which will allow you to continue to live in the community and avoid you having to turn to institutional care. The scheme also provides grants to disabled people leaving hospitals or care homes and establishing themselves in the community. It covers costs like the purchase of household items and furniture or removal expenses and is also available to any disabled person where the grant would relieve an exceptional stress on your family. To apply ask at your local social security office for claim form SF 300.

Interest-Free Loans
Part of the social security scheme (called the Social Fund) operates interest-free loans to people who have received income support for 6 months or more. Loans are available to meet the costs of a range of items and services and are repaid by deductions from social security benefits. If you have a need for a particular item you should first try for a lump sum payment (see above) and if you are refused the social fund officer will automatically consider you for a loan instead.

GROUP E BENEFITS

What are the Group E benefits?
In recent years the Government has moved the responsibility for paying certain benefits away from social security offices and over to employers. There are now two benefits which are paid by employers to members of staff rather

than having to be claimed from social security offices. These are statutory sick pay and statutory maternity pay.

Should I claim statutory sick pay?

Yes, if you become incapable of work while you are an employee. Under the old system you would have claimed sickness benefit when you first became ill or disabled but now you claim statutory sick pay (SSP) from your own employer instead.

You must tell your employer you are incapable of work and (if required) supply supporting evidence such as a letter or certificate from your doctor. Your employer will then pay statutory sick pay (SSP) at rates set down by the Government. Payments will be made in the same way as your wages (and tax and National Insurance contributions will be deducted).

If your employer has a sick pay scheme you will receive SSP plus the difference between SSP and any greater amount due under the scheme.

After 28 weeks of continuous incapacity for work you will be transferred from statutory sick pay to invalidity benefit which is administered by social security (see page 76).

If your employer works out that you are not entitled to SSP or that you are not an employee covered by the scheme, you will be given form SSP 1 (E) to take to the social security office where you can claim sickness benefit instead. Because you would usually be better off on SSP it is worth taking advice if this happens to you. Get in touch with your trades union representative or one of the agencies mentioned in Chapter 11.

Should I claim statutory maternity pay?

Yes, if you are a pregnant woman working for an employer. The benefit is no more generous for disabled than for non-disabled employees. You can get all the details about qualifying conditions for this and the other social security benefits associated with parenthood from the free leaflet FB 8 *Babies & Benefits*, available at your local main post office or any social security office. You need to act promptly as there are time limits for claiming and you could lose money.

BENEFITS GENERALLY

What happens if I am getting a social security benefit and I go into hospital?

I wish I could write that there is a simple straightforward rule that apples to all social security benefits when you go into hospital. The problem is that there is a host of different rules which vary with the length of your stay in hospital and the type of benefit you are receiving.

Ask someone to buy (or borrow) for you the book *Benefits in Hospital* published by the Disability Alliance (address in Chapter 11), which gives all the details. It is well worth checking your position to ensure that you are getting all the financial help you are entitled to at such a difficult time and that you are not going to face a large bill for benefits overpaid when you are discharged.

What happens to my social security benefits if I go abroad for treatment or a holiday?

Once again there is no simple answer. Many social security benefits stop completely if you go abroad; others continue for a short while and yet others are paid indefinitely. The best advice I can give is that you check your position with one of the agencies mentioned in Chapter 11 before you go. If you are travelling to a member state of the European Community you may find that your benefit position is different and that you are entitled to medical treatment free or at a reduced cost.

You can get two helpful leaflets designed for people going abroad and called *Before You Go* (SA 40) and *While You're Away* (SA 41) free of charge from your local social security office.

5. Money Matters

How can I raise my income?

This chapter outlines a number of ways in which you as a disabled person can increase your income. Although many disabled people live on modest incomes there are ways in which everyone can get some more money coming in each week.

If you could raise your income by getting a job or setting up in self-employment, read Chapter 2 which covers help in finding employment or retraining.

If you are already working for an employer or for yourself (or have some other regular source of income) you could raise your income by claiming various tax allowances. These are described later in this chapter.

Whatever your income, you are very probably entitled to one or more of the social security benefits described in Chapter 4. You should read that chapter even if you already receive a social security benefit, because there may be other more generous benefits you can qualify for instead of (or on top of) your present one.

Another option to consider is the possibility of getting an income in the form of compensation for the disability you experience. Chapter 1 sets out the different ways of getting compensation.

How can I pay less tax?

The easiest way to pay less tax is to check what you are paying and ensure that you are only paying the correct amount of tax on properly taxable income. It might be that a 'tax-check' will show that you are paying too much tax or that you are being charged for income tax on non-taxable income. The *Tax Saving Guide* (issued with

Which? magazine by the Consumers' Association) shows you how to check your tax step by step and is kept by most local libraries.

The next way to cut your income tax bill is to claim your entitlement to various *allowances*. These will reduce the tax you have to pay and could mean you pay no tax at all. The full legal details of all the allowances are quite complex so what I have written here is only a very brief summary. More details are available in leaflet IR 22 *Income Tax – Personal Allowances*, published by the Inland Revenue and available free of charge from your local tax office (address in the telephone book under Inland Revenue). The main allowances specifically geared to the disabled are:

Blind Person's Allowance
If you or your spouse are registered as blind with the local authority you qualify for an allowance. If both you and your spouse are blind you get a double allowance.

Live-in Carer's Allowance
If someone lives in your home as a housekeeper and you are a widow or widower, you could get an extra allowance. The housekeeper could be employed by you or might be a friend or relative. This allowance cannot be claimed for tax years after April 1988 but can be claimed for any of the six years before that (see below).

Disabled Wife Allowance
If you are a married man and your wife is disabled you may be able to claim an additional personal allowance if you are bringing up children. To qualify, the tax office must accept that your wife is 'incapacitated' and remains so throughout the tax year such that she cannot help you in looking after the children.

Disabled Dependants Allowance
If you have been supporting a relative who is on a low income you may have qualified for an extra allowance (even if the relative does not live with you). This allowance cannot be claimed for tax years after April 1988 but can be claimed for any of the six years before that.

Each of these allowances is worth hundreds of pounds each year so if you think you even *might* be entitled it is well worth making inquiries. If you have just realized you have been missing out on an allowance don't panic – you can have the allowance backdated for the last six tax years – but do apply straight away.

As a tax payer you can also qualify for the other allowances available to all tax payers (for marriage, old age, widowhood, lone parenthood, etc.). You can check that you are receiving the appropriate allowances by doing a 'tax-check' (see above) or by asking one of the agencies mentioned in Chapter 11 for help with your tax.

To claim the allowances just write to the tax office and put down why you think you might be entitled. It will help them if you give them your tax reference number if you know it.

For details of exemption from *road tax* for car users see page 111.

How can I reduce my housing costs?
You might qualify for help towards meeting the cost of:

    (a) mortgages and home improvement loans
    (b) rent and service charges
    (c) general rates
    (d) community charge (see page 101 for exemptions)

Each of these forms of help is easy to claim and usually more generous because you have a disability. The type of help you can get depends on your housing circumstances and each type is outlined in Chapter 3 – owner-occupiers (page 32), private tenants (page 40), council tenants (page 46) and housing association tenants (page 45).

How can I reduce the cost of my medical treatment?

If your treatment involves travelling to a hospital or clinic see page 114 where I describe the help available with travel costs.

If you are on a modest income you can qualify for all of the following free or at a reduced charge:

(a) NHS prescriptions
(b) dental treatment
(c) glasses
(d) wigs and fabric support
(e) milk for a child (aged up to 5) or a disabled child not at school (aged up to 16).

You will find the details in leaflet AB 11 *Help with NHS Costs* (from larger post offices or any social security office). If you receive the benefits income support (page 80) or family credit (page 79) you will automatically qualify and just need to tell the dentist or optician before you have treatment. If you are on a different low income (whether benefits or earnings) you claim by filling in a form AG 1 which you can collect at a hospital or doctor's or dentist's surgery. If you have already paid for the item or treatment put your claim in as soon as possible.

Most people qualify for this sort of help so you should certainly apply. (Some types of medical condition themselves qualify you for free prescriptions automatically – there is a list in leaflet AB 11 (see above)).

How can I reduce my fuel bills?

As a result of your disability you might well have higher

than average fuel bills – possibly because you are at home a lot or you require more heat than a non-disabled person. Whatever form of fuel you use there are ways of cutting the bills and making them easier to pay.

A first step is improving the insulation of your home so that it better retains the heat you use and therefore cuts your fuel bill. Even the simplest measures can help. You can get the leaflet *Insulation* (DMFF 2) free from the Energy Efficiency Office, Department of Energy, Thames House South, London SW1P 4QJ. Before you start any insulation work (or call in contractors to do it for you) consider whether you qualify for a *Loft Insulation Grant*. These are paid by your local Borough or District Council and can cover up to 90% of your costs if you are receiving income support (page 68), family credit (page 79), or housing benefit (page 88). You get the application form from your local council.

If you are unable to do the work yourself and would prefer not to have the work done by a private contractor there may be a *neighbourhood energy action group* in your area that could insulate your home and help you claim the grants available. You can get the address of the local group by writing to Energy Projects Office, 2 Bigg Market, Newcastle upon Tyne; or telephoning them on 091 261 5677.

Bills are often difficult to pay because they require a lump sum of money to be readily available. If you would prefer to pay regularly towards the cost of your fuel the Gas or Electricity Boards will agree an arrangement with you or supply a 'pay as you go' meter. You just have to write or telephone your local showroom and they will provide details of all the available alternatives to quarterly bills.

If you already have a bill that is difficult to meet, let the supplier know immediately so that you don't get cut off. Then get some advice from one of the agencies mentioned in Chapter 11 about how you can increase your income to clear the bill. If the reason you are in difficulties is because of a low income, get the leaflet *Paying Electricity and Gas Bills* which is available free from Board showrooms and Citizens Advice Bureaux.

Can I get help with paying water rates?
There is no specific help available towards water rates and charges even if you are getting income support or housing benefit. But check that you are not paying water rates on any adaption or extension to your home that has been added because of your disability. Since 1987 a law has exempted such extra property from water rates.

Can I get urgent financial help?
If you need money urgently you can usually make a claim for one or more of the social security benefits described in Chapter 4. But these take time to come through or you may not be entitled under the qualifying conditions. If you are in urgent need you could apply to the local social security office for a 'Crisis Loan'. This will be awarded by a Social Fund Officer if she or he is satisfied that your health will be at risk unless you are loaned some money (e.g. you urgently need an overcoat in bad weather). You will be asked to agree arrangements for a repayment.

Do I have to pay the community charge (or 'poll tax')?
Most disabled people have to pay the community charge. If you are in one of the following categories however you will be 'exempt':
 (a) you are a hospital in-patient and the hospital has become your normal home *or*
 (b) you live in a residential care or nursing home or a hostel which provides care *or*
 (c) you are 'severely mentally impaired'

A person will only come into the last category if they: have a permanent mental handicap (from birth or as a result of injury); and they are receiving invalidity benefit, severe disablement allowance, or are over pensionable age.

If you think you, or someone living with you, might qualify for exemption write to the Registration Officer (your local town hall or library can give you the address). If you are refused exemption you can appeal to an independent tribunal.

6. Disabled Children & Young People

I have a disabled child living with me. What are my rights to extra help with the costs of his or her upbringing?

Raising children is always expensive and all the more so if the child has a disability. There are several grants, benefits and allowances available to help you with the cost of raising your disabled child. Check through the following list and make sure you are getting all the help available:

(a) *child benefit.* This is the weekly benefit available to help with the cost of raising any child (it used to be called family allowance). If you are not already claiming it, get leaflet CH 1 from your local main post office or social security office. Child benefit lasts from birth to age 16 (or up to 19 if the child stays in full-time education).

(b) *family credit.* This is a weekly benefit paid if you (or your partner if you have one) are working more than 24 hours a week and raising a child. For all the qualifying conditions and how to claim see page 79.

(c) *income support.* This is another weekly benefit but paid only where neither you nor your partner has a full time job. All the details and other conditions are given on page 80. You will get extra income support if your disabled child meets the conditions for a disabled child premium (see page 85).

(d) *other benefits.* Your child may be entitled in their own right to a variety of other social security benefits which you can claim for the child and which will be paid to you. Check through Chapter 4 of this book to see what other benefits are available and put in a claim for any your child might be entitled to.

What help can I get with the actual extra expenses of bringing up a disabled child?

There is a special pool of money called the *Family Fund* which exists just to meet the costs and expenses of raising severely physically or mentally disabled children. You can apply to the fund for whatever financial help you need. This might be money for toys, equipment, clothing, footwear, a family holiday or anything else.

Write to the Family Fund, at PO Box 50, York YO1 1UY for an application form. If you return the application form a social worker from the fund will call to discuss your needs in greater detail and report back to the fund. You will then be sent the decision.

If you are refused help or think you have been given less than you need you can apply again and if still refused you can appeal to the Fund's Management Committee. Ask one of the agencies mentioned in Chapter 11 if they can help with the appeal.

Will my child get any extra help or support at school?

Yes. The local education authority have a legal duty to cater for any special educational needs your child may have and, where possible, to provide for these needs in an ordinary school setting. All the details of how to ensure your child gets the appropriate help are given in a booklet called *The Special Education Handbook*, published by the Advisory Centre for Education, 18 Victoria Park Sq., London E2.

What happens when my child reaches 16?

Your child reaching the age 16 is relevant to both the financial arrangements in your household and the education your child is entitled to receive. Because it is so important, there is a free booklet about your child reaching 16 (*After 16 – What Next?*) available from the Family fund (see above for the address).

What income will my child be entitled to at 16?

At the age of 16 a young person becomes eligible to claim a number of benefits in his or her own right. The general conditions for all the main benefits are set out in Chapter 4 but for a young person just reaching 16 the following benefits should be considered particularly:

(a) *severe disablement allowance* (page 70): a young person who is incapable of work will qualify from the age of 16. If he or she is staying at school between 16 and 19 this will affect entitlement to SDA only if more than 21 hours of lessons or other supervised study a week are taken. If the young person receives more than 21 hours' teaching a week, seek the help of one of the agencies mentioned in Chapter 11 as it may still be possible to get the allowance.

(b) *income support* (page 80): at the age of 16 a disabled teenager can claim income support. If he or she stays on at school, income support can still be paid as long as the disability means that even if the young person left school at that age he or she would be unlikely to get a job for at least a year.

If you are not sure which of these benefits is more appropriate to your child's circumstances, help them to claim them both. The social security office will then work out the correct entitlement.

(c) also at 16 any *attendance allowance* you have been receiving for your child will be reviewed. This can sometimes mean that attendance allowance which has been in payment for as long as 14 years is suddenly stopped. If you think the conditions for eligibility described on page 66 are still fulfilled you should apply for a review of the decision. For how to do this and help with it see page 67.

Will the local education authority stop providing schooling at 16?

No. Just like any other child a disabled youngster has the right to stay on at school until the completion of schooling at the age of 18 or 19. If your education authority says they have no places for disabled young people aged between 16 and 19 contact the Advisory Centre for Education for help and advice. Their address is on page 136.

7. Travel & Leisure

A. TRAVEL

As a disabled person what help can I get with travel costs?

Your disability can often mean that you find it more difficult to use private or public transport or have to pay more in fares and travel expenses than a non-disabled person. In this chapter I outline some of the various ways of getting help, in cash and kind, with travel and transportation. Scan through it to find the parts of most help to you then get some more detailed advice about following up those schemes. Where possible I give a reference to an explanatory leaflet or booklet or to an advice service which can offer more help.

If you want more details about all the available schemes before you make a choice get the booklet called *Door to Door* by sending off to The Department of Transport, FREEPOST, Ruislip, MIDDX HA4 0BR. The booklet is free (you don't even have to pay postage to get it) and it provides a wealth of information which I do not have the space to reproduce here.

Can I get help from the tax or benefit systems with the cost of travel?

The social security system has two benefits designed to help meet travel costs. These are: *mobility allowance* and *war pensioners mobility supplement* (see below for more details).

There is also a separate scheme which is part of the benefits system and which helps with the cost of fares to and from hospitals (see below). There is another for fares to a funeral (see below).

You can get more details about help with mobility through the social security system from the free leaflet HB 4 *Help with Mobility* (from social security offices).

The income tax system provides no special help with travel costs in addition to the ordinary allowances available to disabled people (see Chapter 5) but there is a scheme for exemption from road tax (see below).

Do I qualify for mobility allowance?
Yes, if your disability means that you cannot walk, or find it very difficult to walk. The allowance is worth more than £1000 a year so it is well worth claiming. All the details are given in Chapter 4 at page 69. If you think you might be entitled put in a claim. It costs nothing to apply.

Do I qualify for war pensioners mobility supplement?
Yes, if you are a war pensioner and have difficulty walking as a result of a disability you suffered during military service (or which was made worse by military service). You get a weekly tax-free allowance (which takes the place of and is higher than the ordinary mobility allowance) and you can claim at any age. Leaflet MPL 153 gives all details and you can get a copy from your local War Pensioners Welfare Office. If you are thinking about claiming the supplement, see Chapter 2 (pages 9–11) which outlines the help available to disabled people injured during military service.

Can I get a free vehicle from the Government?
There used to be schemes under which disabled people could qualify to have a trike or small car provided by the Government (there was even a special scheme for war pensioners). But it is no longer possible to join these schemes although there are several thousand disabled

people who still have trikes and cars which were first awarded years ago. The idea is that the mobility allowance and mobility supplements already described provide the necessary help in cash or in kind.

If you do not already have your own vehicle, there are various ways you might get help to buy one (see below).

Do I have to give back a Government vehicle I already have?

No. If you were awarded a car or trike under the old scheme you can keep it. If you have a *car* you can transfer to mobility allowance when it becomes unroadworthy or at any other time. The conditions and details are in leaflet NI 255 (free from your social security office).

If you have a *trike* you can have it repaired or replaced as long as spares remain available. You too can switch to mobility allowance (or you could draw the allowance while you take driving lessons for a car). Again, all the details are in social security leaflet NI 255.

As an alternative to switching to mobility allowance you might be able to buy your own car from a government office (see below).

The rules are slightly different if you got the vehicle under the scheme for war pensioners. If you need advice about that, consult your War Pensioners Welfare Office.

What help is available for buying my own car?

Several schemes are available, mostly geared to helping people who receive mobility allowance or supplement meet the cost of purchasing their own car. You can get free information about what is available from the *Mobility Advice & Vehicle Information Service* which is run by the Department of Transport (write to them at TRRL, Crowthorne, Berkshire RG11 6AU). The Department also publishes all the details in a booklet, *Ins and Outs of Car Choice* (from Publications Sales Unit, Building 11,

Victoria Road, South Ruislip, Middx). The Department of Transport's own Disability Unit is at room S10/21, Department of Transport, 2 Marsham Street, London SW1P 3EB (tel: 01 276 5255).

The schemes range from straightforward manufacturers' discounts and help with commercial hire purchase agreements to the Motability Scheme (see below).

If you already have a car or trike under the old Government scheme (described above) there is an arrangement under which you can buy a surplus government car instead of switching to mobility allowance. For the details write to DSS (for England and Wales) at Disablement Services Procurement, 4 Government Buildings, Warbrek Hill Road, Blackpool FY2 0UZ; or SHHD (for Scotland) Room 205, St Andrew's House, Edinburgh EH1 3DE.

What is Motability?

This is a voluntary organization geared to helping people who receive mobility allowance or supplement to hire or buy their own transport. It is open not only to those receiving the benefits but also to the parents of children who receive mobility allowance. The scheme covers:

(a) new cars
(b) used cars
(c) electric wheelchairs
(d) buying outright
(e) buying on hire purchase
(f) leasing

For an application form and more details of the help available contact Motability, 2nd Floor, Gate House, The High, Harlow Essex CM20 1HR.

Do I have to pay car tax?

Some disabled people qualify for relief from the tax

payable on a new car. You will not have to pay car tax if:

(a) you lease a car from Motability or a similar organization *and*

(b) you receive mobility allowance or supplement *and*

(c) the lease is for at least three years.

Nor will you pay VAT on the cost of leasing.

What help can I get with road tax?

You could get exemption from paying the road tax, which is the amount you pay for your tax disc (officially it's called Vehicle Excise Duty). You qualify for exemption if:

(a) you have a car or trike under the old Government scheme (see above) *or*

(b) you get mobility allowance or mobility supplement *or*

(c) you get attendance allowance

If you get *mobility allowance* or *supplement* the vehicle may be your own or you may nominate someone else for exemption. The car should be used for your purposes as a disabled person. That doesn't mean you have to be the only user but if you are not travelling the car should be being used on your behalf for some purpose related to your disability (e.g. to collect medicines or to fetch shopping). The exemption certificate should be sent to you automatically with your mobility allowance award. If you don't have one, write to the Mobility Allowance Unit (or the War Pensioners Mobility Supplement Section) at North Fylde Central Office, Norcross, Blackpool FY5 3TA.

If you get *attendance allowance*, you will qualify for an exemption certificate if you cannot drive for yourself and you are over 65 (or aged between 2 and 5). You must also have difficulty walking and be the registered owner of the car concerned (which must itself be mainly for your own use). If you think you might fulfil all these conditions write for an exemption certificate to DSS (for England and Wales) at Disablement Services Procurement, 4 Government Buildings, Warbrek Hill Road, Blackpool FY2 0UZ; or SHHD (for Scotland) at Room 205, St Andrew's House, Edinburgh EH1 3DE.

Once you have the exemption certificate take it or send it to your local Vehicle Licensing Office (address in the phone book) together with your motor insurance certificate, car registration document and tax disc renewal form. They will then issue a 'tax exempt' disc. If they refuse to issue a free disc you could write to the head office at DVLC (Room 9) Swansea, SA6 7JL and ask for your application to be reconsidered.

Remember, if you are claiming exemption because of mobility allowance the car does not have to be your own. You can nominate a person whose car you use (this might be a relative or even a company you work for). If you later get or use your own car the exemption will revert to you.

What is the Orange Badge Scheme and how can I qualify?

The Orange Badge Scheme provides an exemption from normal parking restrictions for some disabled people. If you display an official orange badge you can park a car which you have used as driver or passenger:

(a) at parking meters free of charge and without time limit

(b) on yellow lines for up to two hours

(c) indefinitely in areas where parking is normally limited to certain times or periods

but you cannot park

(a) in bus lanes

(b) where there is a ban on loading or unloading

You must not only display the badge clearly but also show on it the time of arrival.

The badges are issued by the local council for the area where you live (apply to the local District or Borough Council although the very centre of London is exempt from the national scheme). They can only make a nominal charge for issuing the badge. To qualify you must be:

(a) registered as blind (page 119) *or*
(b) getting mobility allowance or mobility supplement *or*
(c) using a vehicle supplied under the old Government Scheme (see above) *or*
(d) suffering from a 'permanent and substantial' disability which causes inability to walk or very considerable difficulty with walking.

A badge can be issued for a child aged 2 or more if she or he meets these conditions.

If the council refuse to issue you with a badge seek the help of your local councillor. If you think your application has been wrongly rejected you can complain to the local Ombudsman. A local Citizens' Advice Bureau or one of the other agencies mentioned in Chapter 11 will have the complaint form and be able to help you fill it in.

What other help and information can I get about running my own car?

Don't forget that if you have a garage or carport for your car and you need the use of a car because of your disability you could qualify for rate relief (see page 37).

For other straightforward advice and information about motoring as a disabled person you could contact and perhaps join the *Disabled Drivers Association* which has local branches (write to DDA, 18 Creekside, London SE8 3DZ). Or there is a national *Disabled Drivers Motor Club* at Cottingham Way, Thrapston, Northants (tel: 08012 4724).

For written information, ask for a publications list from RADAR, 25 Mortimer St, London W1N 8AB. They publish a guide called *Motoring & Mobility for Disabled People* and 10 individual factsheets on different aspects of mobility for the disabled. For the older disabled person Help the Aged have a free leaflet on mobility (send a stamped addressed envelope to 16/18 St James's Walk, London EC1R 0BE).

If you are looking for more specific information about adapting your car or buying an adapted vehicle, the *Disabled Living Foundation* (380 Harrow Road, London W9 2HU) have regularly updated information sheets. You could also ring or write for specific advice to *Mobility Information Service* (Unit 2a, Atcham Industrial Estate, Upton Magna, Shrewsbury SY4 4UG (tel: 0743 77489).

What help can I get with travelling by rail?
British Rail provide a discount scheme to help disabled people meet the costs of travel and they also provide practical help on request.

The *discounts* are available with a disabled persons railcard. This lasts for one year at a time and allows you and a companion to travel at reduced fares for a single annual payment. You can qualify if you are:

(a) registered blind or partially sighted (pages 119–123) or

(b) deaf (with or without speech) *or*

(c) getting attendance allowance (page 66) or constant attendance allowance (page 29) *or*

(d) getting mobility allowance (page 69) or mobility supplement (page 107) *or*

(e) getting War Disablement Pension for more than 80% disability (page 10) *or*

(f) buying or leasing through Motability (page 110) or

(g) still in possession of a car or trike under the old Government scheme (page 107).

The full details about getting your card and what it entitles you to are in the free leaflet *Disabled Persons Railcard* which you can get at your local British Rail station or by post from the Customer Services Officer, BR, 240 Pentonville Road, London N1 9JZ. It contains the application form.

On the *practical* side, British Rail positively invites disabled people who have mobility difficulties to let them know when they are travelling so that help can be arranged. You can get the details of available help, including staff escorts, free use of wheelchairs and concessionary parking places at stations, from the free leaflet *British Rail and Disabled Travellers* available from your local station or by post from the address given above.

What help can I get with travel by other public transport?

Most local authorities have schemes under which local disabled people can use public transport services such as buses at reduced charges or free. Many of these depend on you being registered with the council as a disabled person. More details about this are given on page 129.

Your local library or main post office will be able to give you details about the local scheme for bus passes and other fares schemes.

What help can I get with the costs of travelling to a hospital or clinic?

If you are on a modest income you probably qualify for help with the financial costs of travelling to hospital if you need to do so. You can get help with travel costs incurred:

- (a) by you travelling to hospital for your own treatment or an appointment
- (b) by a companion needed to accompany you
- (c) by you and your child travelling to hospital for your child to be treated

(d) in travelling home for short leave if you are an in-patient.

You can qualify for full reimbursement of your expenses in one of four ways. Either:

(i)   you are getting income support (see page 80) *or*
(ii) you get family credit (see page 79) *or*
(iii) you are on a low income *or*
(iv) you are a war disablement pensioner (see pages 9–11)

To claim repayment call at the hospital reception. If you are getting income support or family credit just show the receptionist your book and give details of your fares. If you want to claim because you are on a low income ask for form H 11 (they should have a stock at the hospital) and ask the receptionist to complete the 'official inform-ation' part of it. If you are a war pensioner the local War Pensioners' Welfare Office will tell you how to claim.

You will usually get your full fares by public transport repaid. If you travel by car you get an allowance for petrol up to the equivalent of the public transport fare. You can only get the costs of a taxi if there is no public transport route to the hospital or you are physically unable to use public transport because of your disability.

If you apply for help on the basis of low income but your income is too high for free fares you may still get help towards the cost of some of your travel.

Is there any other financial help available towards travel costs?

If you receive income support (page 80) you can claim grants towards the costs of travel from the *Social Fund*. These payments are called community care grants and they do not have to be repaid. There is no exhaustive list of the types of travel expenses that can attract a grant but the following examples are included in the guidance that the benefit officer will use in deciding whether to award a grant:

(a) fares to travel to your new home or when moving from one home to another

(b) fares to visit someone who is ill

(c) fares to attend a relative's funeral

(d) fares necessary following a 'domestic crisis' (e.g. to allow you to travel to stay with relatives).

You apply on form SF300 which you can get from your local social security office by visiting or telephoning. If you have any savings over £500 you will be expected to use some of that to help towards the travel costs. Whether you receive a grant or not depends on the decision of the Social Fund Officer.

If you are refused or get less than you had hoped for, take advice from one of the agencies mentioned in Chapter 11.

Whether or not you are receiving income support you could ask the social services department of your local Regional or County council to help you meet travel costs. They can provide financial help with travel in just the same way as they can towards the cost of holidays and other leisure facilities (see below).

B. LEISURE AND HOLIDAYS

How can I find out about leisure and holiday activities suited to a person with my disability?

A good place to start is with the organization RADAR (address on page 135) who can supply lists of holiday companies and tour operators geared to meeting the specific requirements of disabled people.

Can I get help with meeting the costs of leisure activities and holidays?

You may well find that admission charges to leisure or

recreational facilities are waived or reduced on account of your disability. Some local authority services and facilities for which charges are made can be provided free if you are registered as disabled with that authority (see page 129).

If you need financial help to meet the costs of an outing or holiday, apply in good time to the social services department of your local County or Regional council. They have power to supply holidays or outings themselves and can make contributions towards the costs of holidays arranged independently.

If they find that you have a need for a holiday the Social Services Department will be under a legal duty to consider help with the cost. A case decided in 1984 said that it makes no difference whether the council has arranged or sponsored the holiday themselves or you arrange it privately.

8. Visual Impairment

Does being blind or partially sighted qualify me for benefits or services beyond those for all disabled people?

There are some aspects of our systems of law, social services and social security that give special recognition to the particular difficulties experienced by those with a disablement of blindness or partial sight. The main ones are outlined in this chapter but I can't cover all of the benefits and services available. A very good guide is the *In Touch Handbook* available in braille and on cassette. For details write to *In Touch Handbooks* at PO Box 7, London W3 6XJ. If you would prefer to consider a range of publications before buying one you could contact the National Library for the Blind at Cromwell Road, Bredbury, Stockport SK6 2SG and ask to join their lending scheme for materials in braille, Moon or large print.

Don't forget, if you are not sure whether any special provision is made for those with a visual impairment in any particular scheme of benefit or assistance, the golden rule is to ask!

Is any special help available in getting or keeping a job?

Chapter 2 describes the special assistance available to all disabled people in looking for work or coping with employment. If you are blind or partially sighted you may be particularly interested in the personal reader service (for the part-time help of a reader at work) and/or special equipment to make your work easier in the light of your disability (see page 21).

You should ask the Disablement Resettlement Officer at your local Job Centre about other help available with employment and training.

Is there any special help in the social security system?

The way the benefits system is available to all people with disabilities is outlined in Chapter 4.

If you are blind or partially sighted you may find it easier to qualify for some benefits or you may be automatically entitled to some of them. All the benefits mentioned in Chapter 4 are open to you to claim. The following list contains the main benefits and the ways in which they are modified for you if you are blind or partially sighted. If there is one you are not already claiming you could get advice about making a claim from one of the agencies mentioned in Chapter 11.

(a) *Income support*: there are three important modifications which will help you qualify more easily for this benefit. First, you will receive the disability premium (page 85) if you are registered as blind or partially sighted or have regained your sight in the last six months (see page 122 on registering as blind). Second, the fact that you have non-dependent adults in your home will be ignored in calculating your income support. Third, you will be allowed to claim income support indefinitely without having to be available for work.

(b) *Severe disablement allowance*: if as part of your claim for SDA you are faced with proving that you are disabled (see page 72), you will automatically pass that test if you are blind or partially sighted. This may make it much easier for you to claim the allowance.

(c) *Mobility and attendance allowance*: no special provision is made within the rules for these benefits but many blind and partially sighted people are able to meet the general conditions. Check through these conditions on pages 69 and 66 and if you think you might be entitled put in a claim.

(d) *Industrial injuries benefits*: if your loss of sight resulted in whole or in part from an accident at work you should be receiving one or more of the industrial injuries benefits described on pages 26–9. If not, read through the general conditions for those benefits and put in a claim.

The Department of Social Security produce a *Guide for Blind and Partially Sighted People* (FB 19) which is available free from your local social security office and is in large print. It describes not only social security benefits but also a range of other services available to those with visual impairment.

Is there any special help with taxes and National Insurance?

Yes. If you or your partner (if you have one) is registered as blind with the local authority (see below page 122) you will be eligible for income tax allowances to set against your income. The allowance is worth more than £10 per week if one of you is registered and £20 per week if you are both registered.

You claim by filling in the appropriate space on your tax return. If you don't get a tax return or it is a long time since you filled one in, you can claim the allowance by writing to your tax office. If you have been registered but failed to claim in the past you should claim straight away and ask the tax office to backdate your allowance. The most they can go back is six years.

Is there any extra help with housing costs?

Yes. If you pay rates, the community charge, rent or any other housing costs you may well be eligible to claim financial help with those expenses through the Housing Benefit scheme described on pages 88–90. Although you must satisfy the normal rules, as a blind or partially sighted person you get two extra sorts of help. First, any non-dependent people in your household are ignored when calculating your benefit although they would normally be taken into account. Second, in working out your benefit you will qualify for a disability premium (even if you have recently regained your sight).

Can I get any extra help as a blind or partially sighted student?

Yes. First, you should contact the National Bureau for Students with Disabilities at 336 Brixton Road, London SW9 7AA (tel: 01 274 0565) for information about the general range of extra help available to disabled students.

Then approach the Education Department at the Royal National Institute for the Blind (address on page 135). They are able to make start-up grants to blind or partially sighted students going to university, college, or taking other sorts of education courses. The grant helps meet the cost of any special equipment or materials you might need.

Is it worth registering as blind or partially sighted with the local council?

The answer is usually – yes. If you have read through the whole of this chapter you will already appreciate that a number of special benefits and allowances are available only to visually handicapped people who are already registered with the local council. It costs nothing to apply to be registered and it is usually well worth doing.

You may find that being registered as disabled also qualifies you for free or reduced-cost public transport and discounts from other expenses (such as the TV licence).

How do I get registered with the local council?

First you get in touch with the local office of the Social Services Department. Social Services Departments are run by the County Council (Regional Council in Scotland) or by your Metropolitan Borough Council. If you are not sure who to approach ask at your nearest town hall or main library for the address of the Social Services Department.

Once you have made contact a social worker will arrange to visit you to take your details and process your application. The social worker should ask if you have any special needs or requirements with which social services can help: for example a home help service.

Can I get any special help from social services?

Yes. You can ask at any time for a social worker (or occupational therapist) to call and visit to discuss your needs. Just contact the Social Services Department.

They have a duty to work out whether you have a need for any particular item such as a telephone or radio or tape recorder. If they find you need a particular item, the law says they must supply it – although they can make a reasonable charge. Obviously, if you are on a low or modest income the 'reasonable charge' is going to be less than the full cost. If you are refused don't lose heart – pages 130–131 tells you how to challenge a decision with the help of one of the agencies mentioned in Chapter 11.

9. Carers & Caring

If I am a disabled person and think I would benefit from personal care from another person, what should I do?

First, if you are not already receiving an *attendance allowance* you should consider claiming it. The allowance is worth more than £1000 a year and you can claim it if you need regular help or someone to be with you to make sure you don't suffer an injury as a result of your disability. You don't need to have a carer already and claiming the allowance is fairly straightforward. All the details are on pages 66–7. There are special schemes of attendance allowance if you are injured at work (see pages 26–9) or in military service (see pages 9–11).

Second, you need to arrange for someone (or several people) to provide the personal care you need. You might consider approaching a friend or relative but you should read on a few more pages because it may be possible to get help with some tasks from the health service or your local council or you could arrange to pay someone to provide the help you need.

What help can my local council provide?

Your local County or Regional Council (or Borough Council in metropolitan areas) has a legal duty to consider what help you need at home. You should therefore contact them (ask for the Social Services Department) and a social worker will call on you to discuss what help can be provided. Most councils have a 'home help' service under which you can be given a certain amount of personal help at home by members of the social services staff. They can also arrange for meals to be supplied to you or for meals to be available for you at a day centre (and transportation to the centre). They can make a reasonable charge for these services.

If you are refused help or find it difficult to meet the charges, seek advice from one of the agencies mentioned in Chapter 11.

What help can the Health Service provide?

The local health authority may be able to supply regular nursing care or other medical help and attention for you at home. If you think your disability means that you could use this sort of help at home ask your doctor about what is available locally and for his or her help in arranging what you need.

If I make a private arrangement for caring can I get financial help to pay my carer?

There are several ways you might qualify for financial help towards paying for the services of one or more carers:

(a) there is the attendance allowance mentioned at the beginning of this Chapter (page 124). That benefit is specifically designed to give you some help with meeting the costs of a carer.

(b) if you employ a carer and you are receiving income support you should probably be getting a *severe disability premium* as part of that benefit. Check your benefit includes this amount in the way explained on page 84. The conditions for qualifying for the severe disability premium are set out in full on page 85.

(c) if you employ a carer and are not already receiving income support you should certainly consider claiming it if you are on a modest income. This is because a severe disability premium may be added to your other income support entitlements and help you qualify. The process for claiming income support is set out on pages 80–81.

(d) you should make an application to the Independent Living Fund for financial help. To qualify you must be getting or have applied for the attendance allowance and need to pay for the services of a carer. The Fund can help you with all or part of the cost. You can get more information and the application forms from the Independent Living Fund, at PO Box 183, Nottingham NG8 3RD.

Does my carer qualify for any financial help or allowances?

If your carer is neither a social services home help nor supplied by the health service, he or she might well be entitled to a weekly benefit called the *invalid care allowance*. The details of that allowance are given on page 68.

If you are receiving attendance allowance or constant attendance allowance the person caring for you should be getting 'Home Responsibilities Protection'. This is a type of 'credit' towards their National Insurance contribution record. It is well worth claiming and all the details are in social security leaflet NP 27 which you can get from the local social security office.

Whether or not your carer claims invalid care allowance or is receiving Home Responsibilities Protection, she or he gets special help in claiming income support, (described on pages 80–88). This special help is given in two ways: first, your carer can be working for you for over 24 hours a week and still claim (although the normal rule is that you cannot claim if you work that many hours); second, your carer is exempt from the requirement to be available for work (i.e. he or she does not need to go to the Employment Office to 'sign on').

Can I get more information about employing a carer or about caring generally?

Yes. There is a National Association of Carers. They can be contacted at 29 Chilworth Mews, London W2 3RG (tel: 01 724 7776). Also, you can get general advice and information from any of the agencies mentioned in Chapter 11.

You will need that help and advice in order to work out proper terms and conditions for your carer and in resolving questions like whether they should live-in and how much they should be paid.

What will happen when my carer takes a holiday or other break from caring for me?

Obviously this needs careful planning as far in advance as possible. There is a very helpful booklet called *Taking a Break* which is available free to you and your carer from the King's Fund, Informal Caring Programme, Newcastle Upon Tyne, NE85 2AQ and it goes over all the possibilities.

You should also ask the local Social Services Department (through your social worker) whether there is a local sitting-in service which would provide cover for your carer when she or he needs to take time off. There may also be a similar service called the Homemaker Scheme under which cover can be arranged if your carer is ill.

10. Help in the Home

My disability means I need to make changes at home. What help can I get with these changes?
If the sort of change you have in mind is something structural (for example, construction or conversion of part of your home) you should turn to Chapter 3 where I describe the help available according to whether you are an owner-occupier (page 35), a private (page 42), council (page 48) or housing association (page 45) tenant.

If the change involves the need for personal care and attention see Chapter 9 which describes the caring services available and ways of meeting the costs of having a carer to help you.

If you require some other sort of help at home – such as the adaptation of some facility or furnishings or the installation of some equipment then read through the following pages of this chapter.

How do I go about getting necessary equipment and aids at home?
First, you need a general idea of what sorts of aids and adaptations are available in view of your disability. The Disabled Living Foundation is a good place to start as they specialize in providing that sort of information. You can write to them at 380/384 Harrow Road, London W9 2HU or telephone on 01 289 6111.

Second, the Social Services Department of your local County or Regional Council (Borough Council in metropolitan areas) has a legal duty to consider and respond to your needs, so you should certainly turn to them for help and advice. You just write to or telephone your local social services office and ask for a social worker to visit and assess your requirements. You can get the address from your nearest town hall or main library. They might arrange for an occupational therapist to visit you as well. That person will have a wide range of experience of the various adaptations and equipment available.

The social worker who calls may well encourage you to apply to join the register of disabled persons if you have not already done so.

Should I register with social services as a disabled person?

Social Services Departments have a legal duty to keep a register of disabled people living in their area. The idea is that this information will help them to better plan their services to meet the needs of the disabled. You can register if they accept you have a 'substantial handicap'. This might be a physical or mental handicap or an illness.

You may find it helpful to register because being 'registered disabled' can sometimes help you qualify for additional facilities and services mentioned in this book.

The social services staff will supply an application form on request and many authorities will issue you with a card or reference number to confirm your inclusion on the register.

Who will supply the aids and equipment I need?

Once you have identified with the social worker or occupational therapist all the things you need to make your home more comfortable or easier to manage, the aids and equipment may be available from a variety of sources.

If the item you need is of a medical nature or is intended to meet a medical requirement, your need is most likely to be met from the Department of Health so you should ask your GP or hospital consultant whether they can supply the item in question. Your own doctor has a list of aids and appliances which are available on prescription. Most specialist aids (for example to help with hearing or sight) can be issued by the specialist units in any hospital you attend in connection with your disability. If your need is for a wheelchair ask your hospital consultant or GP.

If the doctor or hospital cannot or will not supply the item, the duty to supply what you need falls on the social service authority so you should ask the social worker or occupational therapist.

What sort of aids and adaptations can I get?

The Social Services Department must supply you with the aids you need at home for normal daily living. This obviously covers a huge range of items from radios, telephones and televisions to very specialized items that would be useful in view of your particular disablement.

The golden rule is that if you think you would be helped by having a specific piece of furniture or aid at home go ahead and ask for it.

Does my local council have to provide the help and assistance I need?

Yes, but at the outset it is their decision whether you need the item in question. Once they have decided you need the item they cannot refuse it to you just because you cannot pay or they 'don't have the money'.

What if my local council says it can't or won't help me?

You should first ask the person who gave you the decision whether the council itself has a complaints or appeals procedure if applications are refused. If there is such a procedure you should obviously use it.

If you remain dissatisfied see whether your council is in fact matching up to its legal responsibilities by reading *Getting the Best Out of Your Act* which you can get free of charge by sending a stamped addressed envelope to RADAR (address on page 135).

If you think the council is falling short of what is required or acting unfairly in refusing you help, contact your local County or Regional Councillor (Borough Councillor in London and metropolitan areas). You can get his or her address and telephone number from County Hall or from your local library. Ask the councillor to take up your case with the council.

If you are still unhappy contact one of the agencies mentioned in Chapter 11. They can help you challenge the decision of the authority (for example by helping you make a complaint to the local government Ombudsman) and can help you get the Minister for the Disabled to look into the failure of the authority to respond to your needs.

You have no automatic right of appeal to a court or tribunal but in a case in 1986 the High Court decided that if you could show that the council had failed to consider your specific need or had acted totally unreasonably you could get a 'judicial review' of the council's decision. You will need legal advice to do this and you should approach one of the agencies mentioned in Chapter 11.

How can I get my existing equipment modified or adapted?

That depends what sort of equipment needs adapting. If it is something to do with the supply of gas or electricity or making the use of those services, e.g. a modification to a cooker, it is worth contacting the Gas and Electricity Boards.

For appliances which use gas, there is a helpful booklet (in large print) called *Advice for Disabled People* which is also available on cassette tape for the visually impaired. For a free copy (or to arrange a visit by a specialist adviser from the Gas Board) contact the Home Services Department, Room 710, British Gas, 326 High

Holborn, London WC1V 7PT (tel: 01 242 0789). Your local Gas Consumers Council has a free leaflet called *If You Are Elderly or Disabled* which advises on available aids and adaptations. For details of your nearest Gas Consumers Council contact the Head Office at 15 Wilton Road, London SW1V 1LT (tel: 01 931 0977).

For advice about modifications to electrical appliances call your local Electricity Board showroom and ask for the Electricity Council leaflet *Making Life Easier for Disabled People.*

For help with the cost of other modifications ask the social worker from your local Social Services Department.

Can I get any special telephone equipment?
Yes, there are a whole range of special telephones and telephone equipment and appliances. For a free guide to what is available write to British Telecom, Action for Disabled Customers, Room B4036, BT Centre, 81 Newgate St, London EC1A 7AJ (0345 581456 – for local rate calls).

11. Advice & Information

Throughout this book I have suggested that when particular problems or difficulties arise you should seek further advice or information. This chapter contains details of the places which may be able to help.

For General Advice or Information
CITIZENS ADVICE BUREAUX
You can get the address and telephone number of your local bureau from the phone book (under 'C') or from the National Association of Citizens Advice Bureaux (tel: 01 833 2181).

INDEPENDENT ADVICE CENTRES
In many areas there are other independent advice centres as well as citizens advice bureaux. To get the address of your nearest centre contact the Federation of Independent Advice Centres (tel: 01 274 1839).

For Legal Advice
LAW CENTRES
Law centres employ lawyers and can give free legal advice in certain cases. For the address and telephone number of your nearest centre contact the Law Centres Federation (tel: 01 387 8570).

SOLICITORS
If you seek advice from a solicitor you will have to pay privately unless you are eligible for help under one of the Legal Aid schemes. Your local main library or Citizens Advice Bureau will have details of all the solicitors in your area who do Legal Aid work and the type of cases they specialize in.

Advice and Information About Social Security Matters
DEPARTMENT OF SOCIAL SECURITY (DSS)
For official advice and information you can contact your local social security office (address and telephone number in the phone book) or telephone free of charge to Freeline DSS (0800 666 555).

For copies of the DSS leaflets mentioned in this book you can write to DSS Leaflets Unit, PO Box 21, Stanmore, Middx HA7 1AY

INDEPENDENT ADVICE
For independent advice about social security contact the Citizens Advice Bureau or another independent advice centre (see above). Your local council may have a Welfare Rights Service. Ask at the local library or town hall.

INFORMATION ABOUT SOCIAL SECURITY
The best books about rights to social security benefits are available from the Child Poverty Action Group, 1-5 Bath Street, London EC1. Ring them (01 253 3406) and ask for a publications leaflet.

Specialist Advice and Information for Disabled People
The main organizations working with disabled people are listed below. Write to them or telephone for details of the services they offer. Often they will be able to put you in touch with local disability groups or organizations of people with the same disability.

DISABILITY ALLIANCE
25 Denmark Street
LONDON
WC2H 8NJ
(tel: 01 240 0806)

ROYAL ASSOCIATION FOR DISABILITY &
REHABILITATION (RADAR)
25 Mortimer St
LONDON
W1N 8AB
(tel: 01 637 5400)

ROYAL SOCIETY FOR MENTALLY
HANDICAPPED CHILDREN & ADULTS (MENCAP)
123 Golden Lane
LONDON
EC1Y 0RT
(tel: 01 253 9433)

ROYAL NATIONAL INSTITUTE FOR THE BLIND
224 Great Portland St
LONDON
W1N 6AA
(tel: 01 388 1266)

For Advice About Housing Matters
SHELTER
This is a campaigning organization for the homeless and
badly housed. They have regional Housing Aid services
which give advice on individual problems. Ring Shelter
(01 253 0202) and ask for details of your nearest Housing
Aid Centre.

SHAC (LONDON HOUSING AID CENTRE)
Advises on housing problems. Write to SHAC at 189a Old
Brompton Road, London SW5 0AR or telephone 01 373
7276.

HOUSING DEBTLINE
Advises on problems with the financial aspects of housing
(like arrears and other debts). Ring them on 021 359
8501/2 or write to them at 318 Summer Lane,
Birmingham B19 3RL.

Specialist Advice and Information for Older Disabled People
AGE CONCERN
There are many local groups. The national office (tel:01
640 5431) at 60 Pitcairn Road, Mitcham, Surrey CR4
3LL can give you the details of your local group as well as
general advice and information.

HELP THE AGED
St James's Walk
LONDON
EC1R 0BE
(tel: 01 253 0253)

Advice About Education
ACE (ADVISORY CENTRE FOR EDUCATION)
18 Victoria Park Sq
LONDON
E2

NOTES

NOTES

NOTES

NOTES

NOTES

NOTES

NOTES